HEIRLOOM RECIPES

HEIRLOOM RECIPES

Best-Loved Recipes from Generation to Generation

Jennifer Saltiel
EDITOR

RUTLEDGE HILL PRESS ™
Nashville, Tennessee
A DIVISION OF THOMAS NELSON, INC.
www.ThomasNelson.com

Published by Rutledge Hill Press, a division of Thomas Nelson, Inc., P.O. Box 141000, Nashville, Tennessee 37214.

Design by Harriette Bateman

Library of Congress Cataloging-in-Publication Data

Heirloom recipes : best-loved recipes from generation to generation /
Jennifer Saltiel, editor.
p. cm.
Recipes of women who use the iVillage Website.
Includes index.
ISBN 1-4016-0045-X
1. Cookery, American. 2. Cookery, International. I. Saltiel,
Jennifer Rosenfeld. II. iVillage.
TX715.H44 2003
641.5973—dc21 2003000255

Printed in the United States of America
03 04 05 06 07 — 5 4 3 2 1

⁂

Contents

Acknowledgments *vii*

Introduction *ix*

1. Breakfast Dishes *1*
2. Appetizers *11*
3. Main Dishes *25*
4. Pasta, Rice, and Potatoes *61*
5. Soups, Sides, and Salads *83*
6. Breads and Muffins *121*
7. Cookies, Bars, and Candies *133*
8. Cakes, Pies, and Desserts *161*
9. My Heirloom Recipes *207*

Metric Conversion Tables *217*

Index *219*

⁎⁕⁎

Acknowledgments

iVillage would like to gratefully acknowledge the wonderful cooks who make up the Heirloom Recipes community at iVillage.com. The women who have gathered in this online discussion group since July 2000 have shared many delicious recipes and heartwarming stories, regularly swapping family favorites and helping new visitors who come looking for help recreating a dish "just like Grandma used to make." We're pleased to share their family recipes and stories with the world at large. Without them, this book would not exist.

In particular, we'd like to thank Elaine Kurschner and Giovanna Roy, who jointly lead the discussions and recipe swaps in this community, for their invaluable assistance in bringing this book to fruition. As leaders of the Heirloom Recipe community, they help preserve America's traditional recipes on a daily basis by nurturing a committed group of cooks who know that great recipes are more than food on a plate—they're a connection with our past.

Finally, many thanks to Alysia Korelc, who provides guidance and supervision for all of our Food discussion areas, for her assistance in coordinating many details, and to Paige Sarlin, who provided invaluable assistance in transforming the recipe card notes of so many women into a single book.

✷

Introduction

My great-grandmother Sarah was a wonderful cook from Austria who never used a recipe, even when she baked. Instead she would improvise adding whatever ingredients struck her fancy. One of her daughter's favorite desserts was a simple cake made with crisp, tart apples and sweet, golden crust that filled their home with an aroma of cinnamon and butter (recipe on page 174). When she got married, she watched Sarah make it and took notes so that she could bake this treat for her own family. My mother—who in turn learned the recipe from my grandmother—likes telling me this story whenever she makes this dessert.

That's what heirloom recipes are all about—not just an opportunity to eat something delicious, but a way to connect generations of a family together and to keep the memory of loved ones alive. For years, the women of the iVillage online community have been swapping their own family favorites, inviting others into their secret recipe boxes. They have found this to be a wonderful way to get to know about each other's history, culture, and traditions and, thanks to the Internet, a chance to make new friends all over the world. We have gathered 200 of these special recipes in this cookbook for you to enjoy. And, as we know every family has its own heirloom recipes, we've included space for you to record your own at the end of this book.

From Giovanna's Fresh Cinnamon Rolls to Aunt Jewel's Chicken and Dumplings, perhaps some of these special recipes will become part of your family's collection and be treasured for years to come.

—Jennifer Saltiel

★1★

Breakfast Dishes

Nona Rosa's Pepper and Egg Frittata

From the kitchen of Elaine Kurschner

When I was a child, my grandparents lived in a big farmhouse. The kitchen had a wood stove around which everyone gathered. One of my favorite memories is of my grandmother cooking breakfast for my grandfather when he came home from his job as a night watchman. To this day, the aroma of peppers frying brings back the image of her standing at the big black stove making his favorite dish.

2 tablespoons olive oil
2 medium bell peppers, washed, seeded, and chopped
1 medium yellow onion, chopped
1 clove garlic, minced
¼ teaspoon crushed red pepper flakes
Salt and pepper
12 eggs, well beaten
Grated Romano cheese

1. Preheat the oven to 350°.
2. Heat the olive oil in a large, ovenproof skillet, and add the peppers and onions. Sauté until well cooked and soft. Add the garlic, and sauté until the onions and peppers begin to brown. Season with the red pepper and salt and pepper to taste.
3. Add the eggs to the skillet, and cook over medium-high heat. With a metal spatula, gently lift the edges so that the uncooked egg can run under. When the bottom is cooked, place the skillet in the oven. Bake until the top is firm and the bottom is lightly browned. Cut into wedges, and serve with lots of crusty bread, grated cheese to taste, and red pepper flakes.

✶ *Makes 6 servings*

Oven-Baked Spanish Omelet

From the kitchen of C.K.

My father made the most wonderful omelet. The recipe was handed down from my great-grandmother, who moved to the United States from Spain. The basic recipe only has olive oil, potatoes, eggs, and seasonings, but you can add whatever you want to it (such as sautéed vegetables, cubed cooked ham, or cooked, crumbled sausage) and it always turns out beautifully. Traditionally served cold, I love this dish piping hot.

1 tablespoon olive oil
4 large potatoes, peeled and sliced
10 large eggs
Salt and pepper

1. Preheat the oven to 350°.
2. In a small cast iron skillet (or oven-safe skillet) with a lid, heat the oil over medium heat. Add the sliced potatoes, and fry them until they are tender to the point of a fork. Remove from the skillet, and place on paper towels to drain.
3. Beat the eggs in a medium bowl, and season with salt and pepper to taste. Arrange the drained potatoes in three layers on the bottom of the oven-safe skillet. Place over low heat, and carefully pour the seasoned eggs over the potatoes. Cover and cook until the middle is cooked halfway through.
4. Place the covered skillet in the oven, and cook until the omelet is cooked all the way through, an additional 15 minutes. Serve immediately, or allow to cool and then serve.

✶ *Makes 6 servings*

Tomato and Egg on Toast

From the kitchen of H.A.

This recipe comes together in about 15 minutes and uses ingredients that are usually on hand. It is good accompanied by Italian sausage or bacon.

2 tablespoons olive oil
1 medium onion, chopped
2 stalks celery, chopped
1 jalapeño, finely chopped (optional)
2 cloves garlic, finely minced
1 (14-ounce) can seasoned tomatoes (Italian, Mexican, or Cajun)
Coarse salt
Freshly ground pepper
4 large eggs, lightly beaten
4 to 8 slices of bread, sliced and toasted

1. Heat the olive oil in a medium pan over medium heat, and add the onion, celery, and jalapeño. Sauté until the onions are soft and translucent. Add the garlic, and cook for an additional 30 seconds. Add the tomatoes, and cook until the liquid is reduced, about 10 minutes. Season with salt and pepper to taste. Add the eggs, and stir constantly until the eggs are set, about 1 minute. Serve immediately over the toast.

✶ *Makes 4 servings*

Grits and Red-Eye Gravy

From the kitchen of Susan Wicks Smith

In the South, you will hear many versions of how we came up with Red-Eye Gravy. One old tale tells of how a wife who was mad at her husband spilled coffee in the pan and made him eat it. Other stories refer to President Andrew Jackson's cook, who had been drinking corn whiskey the night before he made this gravy. No matter what the source is, this old-fashioned, classic gravy is a Southern favorite that you are sure to love. Use a good salt-cured ham, such as Genuine Smithfield Ham.

1 (16-ounce) box grits
1 or 2 slices salt-cured country ham, uncooked, with fat left on
½ to 1 cup strong black coffee, hot

1. Prepare the grits according to the package directions for 6 servings. Meanwhile, in a skillet over high heat, fry the ham in its own fat until nicely browned on both sides. When it is cooked, transfer the ham to a warm plate, and add the hot coffee to the skillet. Stir to deglaze, and scrape the bottom to dissolve the particles that cling to the bottom and sides. Bring the mixture to a boil and cook for 2 minutes.
2. To serve, make a well in the center of each serving of grits, and fill it with the gravy. Serve immediately with the ham.

✶ *Makes 6 servings*

Cottage Cheese Pancakes

From the kitchen of S.B.

These pancakes fall into the category of strange but great recipes. Old-fashioned dry curds were often used in farm cooking, but I rarely use them these days, except when I make this delicious recipe. Try them. You might like them as much as my family does.

1 cup large-curd cottage cheese
3 eggs
2 tablespoons butter, melted
¼ cup all-purpose flour
¼ teaspoon salt
Butter for griddle or frying pan

1. Drain the cottage cheese in a sieve, pressing it down firmly and letting it stand and drip for about 1 hour.
2. In a medium bowl, beat the eggs well. Add the drained cottage cheese, melted butter, flour, and salt, and mix until just blended.
3. Preheat the frying pan or griddle over high heat. Test the griddle by sprinkling a few drops of water on it. When the water skitters across the griddle, it is ready. Melt ½ teaspoon butter on the griddle, and tilt the pan to coat.
4. Drop the batter by large spoonfuls onto the preheated griddle. Cook until bubbles and small holes form on the surface and the edges are slightly brown, about 2 minutes. With a pancake turner or metal spatula, flip and cook the pancakes until golden, about 1 minute. Repeat with the remaining batter, keeping the finished pancakes warm on a heatproof plate in a 200° oven.

✶ *Makes 4 servings*

Overnight Apple French Toast

From the kitchen of C.G.

In the foothills of Northern California is an area called Apple Hill. It's appropriately named since it is the region where many of the apples in California are grown. This recipe comes from that area. I have tried my fair share of overnight recipes with many soggy bread results, but this is one of my favorite breakfast successes.

½ cup butter, melted
¼ cup honey
2 teaspoons plus ½ teaspoon ground cinnamon
6 eggs
1 cup apple cider
½ teaspoon salt
1 cup milk
¼ cup sugar
1 loaf French bread, cut on the diagonal

1. Combine the butter, honey, and the 2 teaspoons cinnamon in a small bowl. Mix well. Pour into a 10 x 15-inch jellyroll pan. Let stand.
2. In a large bowl, beat the eggs, apple cider, salt, milk, sugar, and the remaining ½ teaspoon cinnamon. Mix well. Dip the bread slices into the egg batter, and place in the prepared pan. Pour any remaining egg batter over the bread. Cover and refrigerate overnight.
3. Preheat the oven to 400°.
4. Uncover the pan and bake, turning the bread over once, until golden brown, about 35 minutes. Top with your favorite syrup, jam, or jelly.

✶ *Makes 4 to 6 servings*

Tried-and-True Sour Cream Coffeecake

From the kitchen of Lee Roff

My mother-in-law gave me this recipe, and it had been in her family for many years. I'm so happy to share it, as it will help keep her memory alive. I've made this for many years, and it never fails to please. It stays moist and travels well, too. Just wrap the cooled cake in plastic wrap and then foil. It's a real treat with a cup of coffee or a cold glass of milk. This makes a large cake, so there will be plenty to wrap.

1 pound butter
2 ½ cups plus 6 teaspoons granulated sugar
4 large eggs
4 ½ cups flour
2 teaspoons baking soda
2 teaspoons baking powder
1 teaspoon salt
2 teaspoons vanilla extract
1 pint sour cream
⅔ cup firmly packed brown sugar
2 teaspoons cinnamon
1 cup walnuts, chopped

1. Preheat the oven to 350°. Grease and flour an angel food cake pan or a large Bundt pan.
2. In a large bowl of an electric mixer, beat the butter, and add the 2½ cups sugar slowly. Beat together until light and fluffy. Add the eggs, one at a time. Blend well. In a medium bowl, sift together the flour, baking soda, baking powder, and salt. In a separate small bowl, stir the vanilla into the sour cream. Add the flour mixture and the sour cream mixture alternately to the butter-sugar mixture. Beat well until smooth.
3. In another small bowl, combine the remaining 6 teaspoons granulated sugar with the brown sugar and cinnamon. Add the chopped walnuts and mix.
4. Pour half the batter into the prepared pan. Sprinkle half of the cinnamon/nut mixture over the batter evenly. Pour the remaining batter over the mixture, and top with the remaining cinnamon/nut mixture. Bake until a toothpick placed in the center of the cake comes out clean, about 1½ hours. Cool before removing from pan.

✶ *Makes 12 servings*

Apple Streusel Coffeecake

From the kitchen of Barbara Kajfasz

I received this coffeecake recipe from a friend about 13 years ago. She called it "good old-fashioned comfort food." I love having this cake with my daughter, Corrine, on dark, cold nights with some tea and conversation.

For the filling:
8 apples
3 packed tablespoons light brown sugar
⅓ cup raisins
Dash of ground cinnamon
¼ cup apple juice or water
2 tablespoons cornstarch (optional)

For the cake:
2 ¼ cups all-purpose flour
¾ cup sugar
¾ cup cold butter, cut into pieces
½ teaspoon baking powder
½ teaspoon baking soda
1 large egg, beaten
¾ cup buttermilk or sour milk

1. Preheat the oven to 350°. Grease a 9-inch springform pan.
2. To make the filling, peel and cut the apples into thin slices. In a saucepan, place the apples, brown sugar, raisins, and cinnamon. Add the apple juice (or water), and bring to a gentle boil over medium-low heat. Set aside to cool. (If the mixture is too watery when it cools, stir in the cornstarch to thicken the filling. Cook for an additional 2 minutes. Set aside to cool.)
3. To make the cake, place the flour and sugar in the work bowl of a food processor. Pulse two times to mix. Add the cold butter. Process until the mixture is crumbly, about 5 or 6 pulses. Set aside ½ cup of the mixture, and transfer the rest of the mixture to a large mixing bowl. To the large bowl, add the baking powder and baking soda. In a small bowl, combine the egg and buttermilk. Add the egg/buttermilk to the dry ingredients, and stir until just moistened.
4. Pour two-thirds of the batter into the prepared pan. Using a rubber scraper or spoon, spread this batter part of the way up the side of the pan. Spoon the apple filling over the batter. Drop spoonfuls of the remaining one-third of the batter over the filling. Sprinkle with the reserved flour/sugar/butter crumb mixture. Bake for 50 minutes.

Note: This coffeecake freezes well.
Variation: Substitute ⅓ cup fresh cranberries for the raisins in the filling. When using cranberries, use apple juice as the liquid to counter the tartness of the cranberries.

✶ *Makes 8 servings*

Christmas Coffeecake

From the kitchen of L.F.

In my family we eat this coffeecake slightly warm on Christmas morning. I make it ahead of time, and I always make six or so times the recipe and give the extra cakes to my friends for their Christmas breakfasts. It's one way that I have found to include more people in my family traditions.

For the cake:

1½ cups all-purpose flour
¾ cup sugar
2½ teaspoons baking powder
¾ teaspoon salt
¼ cup butter
¾ cup milk
1 egg

For the topping:

⅓ cup brown sugar
¼ cup all-purpose flour
½ teaspoon ground cinnamon
3 tablespoons butter

1. Preheat the oven to 350°. Grease and flour a 9-inch round cake pan.
2. To make the cake, in a large bowl of an electric mixer, slowly mix the flour, sugar, baking powder, and salt. Beat in the butter, milk, and egg. Mix well. Pour into the prepared pan.
3. To make the topping, in a separate small bowl, using a fork, combine the brown sugar, flour, cinnamon, and butter. Mix until crumbly. Sprinkle the topping over the batter.
4. Bake until a toothpick inserted in the center comes out clean, about 25 to 30 minutes. The cake tastes best served warm.

✶ *Makes 6 to 8 servings*

Get Up and Go Breakfast Cookies

From the kitchen of C.J.

My kids love these breakfast treats on Saturday mornings when they are fresh from the oven. Always serve them warm with a tall glass of milk.

¼ cup butter at room temperature
½ cup sugar
1 egg
2 tablespoons thawed orange juice concentrate
1 tablespoon grated orange zest
1¼ cups flour
1 teaspoon baking powder
½ cup Grape-Nuts cereal

1. Preheat the oven to 350°.
2. In a large bowl of an electric mixer, beat together the butter, sugar, egg, orange juice concentrate, and orange zest until light and fluffy. Gradually add the flour and baking powder, and beat until blended. Stir in the cereal.
3. Drop by teaspoonfuls 2 inches apart on an ungreased cookie sheet. Bake until the edges are golden, about 10 to 12 minutes. Transfer to a wire rack to cool.

✶ *Makes 20 to 24 cookies*

Appetizers

Nanny's Charleston Pickled Shrimp

From the kitchen of A.M.

My father's mother loves this appetizer. Everyone will rave about it, and you'll find yourself making it over and over again.

6 small white onions
2 pounds large shrimp, boiled and deveined
20 to 25 bay leaves
1 cup salad oil
¼ cup tarragon vinegar
2 teaspoons salt
½ teaspoon dry mustard
1 teaspoon sugar
1 teaspoon Worcestershire sauce
Cayenne
Handful of pickling spices

1. With a sharp knife, peel the onions and cut them into very thin slices.
2. In a gallon jar with a lid, put a layer of boiled shrimp, a layer of bay leaves (about 5 to a layer), and a layer of sliced onions. Alternate layers until shrimp are all used.
3. In a small bowl, whisk together the oil, vinegar, salt, dry mustard, sugar, Worcestershire sauce, cayenne, and pickling spices, mixing well. Pour over the shrimp. Replace the lid of the jar and refrigerate. Marinate for 24 hours. Shake the jar every now and then.
4. Serve with toothpicks in a bowl placed over ice or as a salad with lettuce.

✶ *Makes 8 servings as an appetizer or 6 to 8 servings as a salad*

Stuffed Mushrooms

From the kitchen of L.F.

I make these for my husband and he loves them.

3 (8-ounce) cans tomato sauce
⅓ cup vermouth
1 teaspoon oregano
3 pounds fresh mushrooms, cleaned with stems removed
1 pound hot pork sausage, crumbled

1. Preheat the oven to 350°. Line a baking sheet with aluminum foil.
2. Combine the tomato sauce, vermouth, and oregano in a large saucepan over medium heat. Bring to a simmer, and cook for 5 minutes. Remove from the heat and reserve.
3. Place the mushroom caps on the prepared baking sheet. Stuff each cap with crumbled sausage, pressing firmly down to pack. Bake until the meat is browned and mushrooms have wilted, about 30 minutes. Remove from the oven, and transfer the mushrooms to a saucepan with the sauce. Let the mushrooms marinate for at least 2 hours. Reheat in the saucepan over low heat and serve hot.

* *Makes 6 servings*

Nut-Stuffed Mushrooms

From the kitchen of Elaine Kurschner

I originally had these Nut-Stuffed Mushrooms at a party in the 1960s. When the hostess wouldn't give me her recipe, I experimented until I was able to replicate it myself. It is now one of my favorites.

24 large mushrooms, cleaned
3 tablespoons fresh lemon juice
3 tablespoons water
2 tablespoons butter plus ½ cup soft butter
2 tablespoons finely minced onion
2 cloves garlic, minced
½ cup chopped walnuts, pecans, or almonds
½ cup fine dried bread crumbs
Salt and pepper

1. Preheat the oven to 350°. Line a baking sheet with foil.
2. Remove the stems from the mushrooms, and trim the ends. Place the stems in a small bowl.
3. With a melon-ball scoop or spoon, lightly scoop out a small amount of the center of the mushroom caps. Place the mushroom pieces in a bowl with the stems. In another small bowl, combine the lemon juice and water. Dip each cap into the bowl of lemon water to keep them from turning dark. Sprinkle 1 tablespoon of the lemon water on the stems and pieces as well.
4. With a sharp knife, chop the reserved mushroom stems and pieces. In a skillet over medium heat, heat the butter, and sauté the mushroom pieces, onion, and garlic until soft. Remove from the heat, and set aside to cool.
5. In a medium bowl, mix the chopped nuts, bread crumbs, and softened butter. Stir in the cooled onion mixture. Taste and season with salt and pepper.
6. With a small spoon, stuff the mushrooms with the nut mixture, and place on the prepared baking sheet. Bake for 20 minutes. Serve hot.

∗ *Makes 24 appetizers*

Stuffed Jalapeños

From the kitchen of Marsha Gillet

Everyone just loves these. You will, too.

1 (8-ounce) package cream cheese, softened
12 large fresh jalapeños, halved, deveined, seeded, and washed
1 (1-pound) package thinly sliced bacon, cut in half crosswise

1. Preheat the oven to 350°. Line a baking sheet with aluminum foil.
2. Stir the cream cheese until smooth and creamy in a small bowl. You can also use a mixer. Spoon the cream cheese into each jalapeño half.
3. Wrap the jalapeño with a bacon slice, and secure it with a toothpick inserted through the ends of the bacon and through the whole jalapeño. Place on the prepared sheet, and bake until bacon is crispy, about 10 to 15 minutes.

✶ *Makes 24 appetizers*

Spinach Feta Spread

From the kitchen of H.Y.

5 ounces fresh spinach, cleaned with stems removed
1 tablespoon butter
1 small onion, finely chopped
1 small sweet red pepper, diced
¾ cup light cream cheese, softened
½ cup cottage cheese
2 tablespoons fresh dill, chopped
2 teaspoons lemon zest
Dash of hot pepper sauce
Pinch of freshly ground black pepper
1½ cups crumbled feta cheese

1. Cook the spinach with 2 tablespoons of water in a saucepan over medium-high heat until just wilted, about 4 to 5 minutes. Transfer to a colander, and drain, squeezing out any excess moisture. Chop finely.
2. In a clean saucepan over medium heat, melt the butter, and sauté the onion and pepper until softened, about 5 minutes.
3. In the bowl of a food processor, process the cream cheese and cottage cheese until smooth. Add the dill, lemon zest, pepper sauce, and pepper. Pulse to blend. Add the spinach and the onion and pepper mixture, and pulse until just combined. Transfer to a large bowl, and stir in the feta cheese. Mix well and serve. Can be made 2 days ahead.

✶ *Makes 2 cups*

Cream Cheese and Pineapple Cheese Ball

From the kitchen of M.S.

This appetizer is wonderfully simple and delicious.

2 (8-ounce) packages cream cheese, softened
1 (8-ounce) can crushed pineapple, drained
¼ cup chopped green peppers
2 tablespoons finely chopped onion
1 teaspoon seasoned salt
1 cup chopped pecans

1. Combine the cream cheese, pineapple, green peppers, onion, and seasoned salt in a medium bowl. Mix well. Form into a ball, cover, and refrigerate for about 2 hours.
2. Roll in the chopped pecans, wrap tightly in plastic wrap, and refrigerate overnight. Tastes best when served at room temperature.

✶ *Makes 8 servings*

Best Holiday Cheese Ball

From the kitchen of D.B.

We always serve this cheese ball with Ritz crackers.

4 (8-ounce) packages cream cheese, softened
4 teaspoons Accent seasoning
1 (8-ounce) can chopped mushrooms
1 (8-ounce) can chopped ripe olives
6 green onions, chopped
1 small jar dried beef, chopped
1 to 1½ cups chopped pecans

1. Combine the cream cheese, seasoning, mushrooms, olives, onions, and dried beef in a large bowl. Mix well, and form into 2 large balls.
2. Roll each ball in the chopped pecans, and wrap tightly with plastic wrap. Refrigerate overnight. Serve with crackers.

✶ *Makes 10 to 12 servings*

Pizza Fondue

From the kitchen of Jennifer Degtjarewsky

My mother made this every Christmas Eve. We look forward to it every year. It just wouldn't feel like Christmas without it.

1 package onion soup mix
1 (15-ounce) can tomato sauce
1 tablespoon Worcestershire sauce
1 tablespoon oregano
1½ cups grated Cheddar cheese
1 small loaf French or Italian bread, cubed

1. In a small saucepan over low heat, combine the onion soup mix, tomato sauce, Worcestershire sauce, and oregano. Stir in the cheese. Serve warm with the bread cubes for dipping.

✶ *Makes 3½ cups*

Nanny's Crab Dip

From the kitchen of Stacia Jesner

My paternal grandmother, Nanny, always made this for holiday parties. My mother (and then each of my sisters and I) also adopted it as a staple for entertaining. It absolutely melts in your mouth. Even folks who don't like seafood love this dip. It's perfect served with Triscuits.

1 (6-ounce) can crabmeat, drained
1 (6-ounce) can baby shrimp, drained
8 ounces cream cheese
1 teaspoon lemon juice
¾ cup dried bread crumbs
2 tablespoons butter

1. Preheat the oven to 400°.
2. Mash the crabmeat, shrimp, cream cheese, and lemon juice together in a small bowl.
3. Spread the mixture into a small baking dish. Sprinkle with bread crumbs, and dot with butter. Bake for 45 to 60 minutes or until the dip is bubbly and the topping golden. Serve in the baking dish with Triscuit crackers.

✶ *Makes 2 cups*

Taco Dip

From the kitchen of F.M.

I know there are a zillion versions of taco dip, but this is our favorite. It is very easy to adjust to taste. I've added beans, taco meat, salsa, and guacamole depending on my mood. I like making individual plates of the dip and chips, and serving the toppings buffet style so people can top their plates as desired. I always make the dip itself a day ahead though. I find it tastes better.

8 ounces cream cheese, softened
8 ounces sour cream
1 package taco seasoning
1½ cups shredded lettuce
3 to 4 tomatoes, finely chopped
1½ to 2 cups shredded Cheddar cheese
Tortilla chips

1. Mix together the cream cheese, sour cream, and taco seasoning in a medium bowl.
2. Spread a layer of the dip mixture on a pie plate or on individual plates. Cover with the lettuce, tomatoes, and cheese. Serve with tortilla chips.

✶ *Makes 6 to 8 servings*

Texas Caviar

From the kitchen of A.B.

My sister-in-law's best friend gave her this recipe for an interesting black-eyed pea dip. Now it's a family favorite at all our gatherings.

2 (14-ounce) cans black-eyed peas, rinsed and drained
2 (14-ounce) cans white whole kernel corn, drained
4 or 5 medium tomatoes, chopped
8 to 10 scallions, chopped
2 medium green peppers, seeded and chopped
1 cup chopped onions
1 cup chopped fresh parsley (optional)
2 (8-ounce) bottles Kraft Zesty Italian Dressing
Garlic salt

1. In a large bowl, combine the peas, corn, tomatoes, scallions, peppers, onions, parsley, dressing, and garlic salt to taste. Refrigerate. Keeps for several days.
2. Before serving, drain well. Serve with tortilla chips or Fritos.

✶ *Makes 6 to 8 cups*

Bagel Chips

From the kitchen of Carol Montague

Adjust the seasoning combinations according to your own taste. I like to serve garlic and cheese chips with salad and plain chips with dips and cheeses.

1 bagel
Nonstick cooking spray or olive oil
⅛ teaspoon garlic powder
⅛ teaspoon onion powder
⅛ teaspoon ground cumin
⅛ teaspoon dried oregano
⅛ teaspoon fat-free Parmesan cheese
⅛ teaspoon chili powder

1. Preheat the oven to 400°. Line a baking sheet with aluminum foil.
2. With a sharp knife, slice the bagel into very thin slices so that you can almost see through them (you'll get about 9 slices). Place the slices on the prepared baking sheet. Lightly coat them with nonstick cooking spray or olive oil. Very lightly sprinkle the slices with the garlic powder, onion powder, cumin, oregano, Parmesan cheese, and chili powder. Or leave them plain. Remember, a little seasoning goes a long way.
3. Bake until lightly brown, about 3 to 4 minutes. Watch carefully because the slices burn easily. Remove from the oven, and break each slice into 4 chips.

✶ *Makes about 36 small pieces*

Festive Crostini

From the kitchen of B.K.

This is a great appetizer that can be made an hour before the guests arrive. Last time I made the recipe for a holiday party, the guests could not get enough of the crostini. They are so pretty, too—red and green.

1½ ounces sun-dried tomatoes
1½ cups boiling water
1 baguette, cut into ½-inch-thick slices
1 garlic clove, halved
4 ounces cream cheese, softened
4 ounces feta cheese
1 garlic clove, minced
1 (2½-ounce) can sliced black olives, drained
¼ cup chopped fresh parsley

1. Preheat the oven to 400°.
2. Soak the tomatoes in the boiling water in a small bowl for about 30 minutes. Drain and chop.
3. Arrange the bread on a baking sheet, and bake until toasted, about 10 to 12 minutes. Remove from the oven, and rub each slice with the cut edge of half a garlic clove, using one half-clove for half the slices, and the other half-clove for the rest.
4. In a small bowl, combine the cream cheese and feta cheese. Mix well, and spread evenly on the bread slices.
5. In a separate small bowl, combine the tomatoes, minced garlic, olives, and parsley. Mix well, and spoon over the cheese. Serve at room temperature.

✶ *Makes 30 appetizers*

3

Main Dishes

Chicken Carbonara

From the kitchen of M.J.

One of our standbys is this super-simple recipe. It is so good. We often cut up the chicken into pieces and serve it mixed with bow tie pasta.

1 tablespoon olive oil
4 boneless, skinless chicken breasts
2 small onions, chopped
2 slices bacon or pancetta (Italian bacon), chopped
1 cup fresh or frozen green peas, thawed
⅓ cup dry white wine or chicken broth
1 (17-ounce) jar creamy Alfredo pasta sauce, such as Five Brothers
Cracked black pepper (optional)

1. In a medium-size, nonstick skillet over medium-high heat, heat the oil and brown the chicken. Transfer the chicken to a plate.
2. In the same skillet, cook the onions, bacon, and peas, stirring occasionally, until the bacon is cooked and the onions are tender, about 6 minutes. Add the wine, and cook 1 minute longer. Stir in the Alfredo sauce. Return the chicken to the skillet. Bring the mixture to a boil over high heat. Reduce the heat to low, and simmer covered until the chicken is no longer pink, about 10 to 15 minutes. Sprinkle with cracked black pepper.

* *Makes 4 servings*

Aunt Jewel's Chicken and Dumplings

From the kitchen of D.N.

Every Thanksgiving and Christmas my family makes this traditional recipe. I learned to make it from my mother, who learned it from her mother, my granny. Granny's mother died when Granny was just eight years old, so this recipe was taught to her by her older sister, Jewel. Granny was born in 1899, the youngest daughter of a family of four.

Our family lived in what's now Alabama in the late 1700s before settling in Arkansas. This chicken and dumplings recipe probably made its way along with my family more than one hundred years ago. Granny and Aunt Jewel are both gone, and Mama is getting older. I am the one in charge of making it these days, and I find myself making it quite often.

1 whole chicken, cut into 4 to 8 pieces
2 cups water
3 to 4 cups all-purpose flour
Salt and freshly groung pepper

1. In a large pot over high heat, place the cut-up chicken with enough cold water to cover the chicken by 1 inch. Bring to a boil and cover. Reduce the heat, and simmer until the juices run clear when the chicken is pricked with a fork, about 30 to 45 minutes. Transfer the chicken from the broth to a cutting board, reserving the broth in the pot. Allow the chicken to cool, and then remove the skin and bones. Cut into large pieces, and return to the broth. Keep the broth and chicken simmering while preparing the dumplings.
2. Place the 2 cups water in a medium bowl. With a wooden spoon, stir in enough flour to absorb all the water. Keep adding flour until the mixture forms a large ball of dough that is stiff and dry. (It should not be sticky.)
3. Turn the dough onto a lightly floured surface, and knead lightly. With a sharp knife, cut the ball into quarters. Flatten one of the quarters, and with a rolling pin, roll out one piece into a thin circle about ⅛-inch thick. Starting at one end, roll the dough as if making a jelly roll, and cut across the roll at 1-inch intervals. Repeat with the remaining dough.
4. Place each batch of dough strips into the simmering broth as they are cut, submerging them with a spoon as you add them. Cook the dumplings until they are done, about 10 to 15 minutes. The dumplings will float to the top of the broth when done. Do not allow the liquid to boil over. Add the salt and pepper to taste.
5. With a slotted spoon, transfer the chicken and dumplings into serving bowls. Pour the broth over the top and serve hot.

✶ *Makes 4 to 5 servings*

Baked Chicken and Rice

From the kitchen of Elaine Kurschner

I make so many variations of this dish and rarely do it the same way twice. But here's the basic recipe from which to start.

1 whole chicken, cut into quarters
1 cup Italian salad dressing
3 tablespoons vegetable oil
½ cup minced onion
1 clove garlic, minced
1 cup uncooked rice
2 cups chicken broth or water
¼ cup fresh minced parsley, optional garnish
¼ cup sliced scallions, optional garnish

1. Place the chicken in a bowl, and cover it with the salad dressing. Allow to marinate for ½ hour.
2. Meanwhile preheat the oven to 375°. Remove the chicken from the marinade, and place it skin side down on a greased baking pan. Transfer the marinade to a small saucepan over medium heat. Bring to a boil. Remove from the heat, and reserve for basting.
3. Place the chicken in the oven, and bake for ½ hour, basting with reduced marinade every 10 minutes. Turn the chicken over to allow the skin to brown, and cook for an additional ½ hour, continuing to baste every 10 minutes.
4. Meanwhile, in a medium saucepan, heat the oil, and sauté the onions and garlic until golden. Add the rice, and sauté it until the rice becomes milky white. Add the chicken broth, and bring to a boil. Reduce the heat, cover, and cook until all the liquid is absorbed, about 25 minutes.
5. To serve, spoon the rice onto a large platter, and arrange the chicken on top. Garnish with parsley and scallions.

✶ *Makes 4 servings*

Chicken Paprikás

From the kitchen of C.W.

This recipe has been in my family for many years, and after all this time, I just go in the kitchen and do it from memory. It's one that my family really likes. I often use sliced, boneless, skinless chicken breasts and add extra sour cream for thickness. I also use olive oil in place of the butter.

For the chicken:

4 tablespoons butter
1 onion, chopped
¾ teaspoon black pepper
1 tablespoon salt
3 to 4 pounds chicken parts
1½ cups water
½ pint sour cream

For the dumplings:

2 cups all-purpose flour
2 eggs
½ teaspoon salt
½ cup water

1. To make the chicken, melt the butter in a large pot over medium-high heat, and sauté the onion until browned. Add the pepper, salt, and chicken. Sauté until the chicken is lightly browned, about 10 minutes. Add the water, and bring to a simmer. Reduce the heat, and cook until the chicken is tender. Remove the pot from the heat, and with a slotted spoon, transfer the chicken to a separate plate. Allow the broth to cool slightly, and whisk in the sour cream. Mix well.
2. To make the dumplings, in a medium bowl mix the flour, eggs, and salt. Add enough water to form a smooth dough.
3. Bring a large pot of salted water to a boil. Add a few drops of oil to the water to prevent the dumplings from sticking. Working in batches, drop spoonfuls of dough into the water. Cook until the dumplings float to the top, about 2 minutes. Remove from the water with a slotted spoon and reserve. Continue until all the dough is used.
4. To serve, place the dumplings in the bottom of a dish, cover with the chicken pieces, and pour the sauce over all.

⋆ *Makes 8 to 10 servings*

My Mom's Famous Chicken Squares

From the kitchen of S. T.

When I was a child, I would always request this dinner for my birthday. Now, whenever I make it, I get rave reviews, and people ask me for the recipe. It's certainly not health food, but it is a delicious (and pretty easy) meal that's even good enough for company. I hope you enjoy it as much as my family has.

6 ounces cream cheese
5 tablespoons melted butter
½ teaspoon salt
⅛ teaspoon pepper
3 cups cubed, cooked chicken
3 tablespoons milk
1½ tablespoons chives
2 (8-ounce) packages ready-to-bake crescent rolls, such as Pillsbury's
1 tablespoon melted butter
¾ cup seasoned dried bread crumbs

1. Preheat the oven to 325°.
2. Blend together the cream cheese and butter in a medium bowl. Mix in the salt, pepper, cubed chicken, milk, and chives.
3. Place two of the crescent roll triangles on a cookie sheet next to each another to make a rectangle. Pinch together the dough "seams." Repeat with all of the crescent roll dough to form 8 separate rectangles. Place the chicken mixture in the center of each rectangle, dividing the mixture evenly among all the rectangles. Pull up the corners of each rectangle and seal, and make a little knot with the four corners. Pinch together any open gaps in the dough.
4. Brush each package with the melted butter, and sprinkle with the seasoned bread crumbs. Bake until golden, about 30 minutes.

✶ *Makes 8 chicken squares, 4 servings*

Daddy's Mozzarella Chicken

From the kitchen of A.B.

Daddy created this recipe for my mother right after they were married. Once my sister, Katherine, and I came along, he expanded the recipe, and now it serves a whole family. A simple, one-dish recipe, it requires very little cleanup, which is clearly one reason why my mom liked it. The other reason is that it is extremely delicious. In my family, we love tons of onions and sour cream, but if you like less, the recipe will still taste great. You can use half the amount of mozzarella if it's too rich for you.

2 tablespoons butter
2 large onions, cut into 1-inch strips
2 large green peppers, cut into 1-inch strips
3 boneless, skinless chicken breasts, cut into bite-size chunks
2 (16-ounce) cans diced tomatoes, drained
8 ounces sour cream
16 ounces mozzarella cheese, grated

1. Melt the butter, and sauté the onions, green peppers, and chicken in a large skillet over medium-high heat. Cook until the peppers and onions are soft and chicken is just cooked through. Add the tomatoes, cover, and cook until bubbly, about 20 minutes. Reduce the heat to low, add the sour cream, and slowly cook until thickened, about 5 to 10 minutes. Do *not* boil.
2. Sprinkle the cheese over the chicken and vegetables. Remove the skillet from the heat, and cover the skillet until the cheese melts. Serve with or without rice.

✶ *Makes 4 servings*

Green Noodle Chicken Casserole

From the kitchen of L.J.

The dean of students made this dish for a Christmas lunch we had for our school staff. People were talking about it for weeks. It's easy, slightly different, and tasty.

2 tablespoons butter
1 large onion, diced
1 pound mushrooms, sliced
1 to 2 teaspoons curry powder
2 (10½-ounce) cans cream of mushroom soup
2 cups sour cream
½ cup chicken broth
6 ounces spinach noodles, cooked according to directions on package
3 cups cooked chicken, diced
1 tablespoon Worcestershire sauce
Salt and pepper
1 teaspoon oregano
1 cup grated Monterey Jack cheese

1. Preheat the oven to 350°.
2. Melt the butter, and sauté the onions in a large skillet over medium-high heat until they begin to soften. Add the mushrooms and curry powder, and sauté until the mushrooms begin to soften. Add the soup, sour cream, and chicken broth. Stir well. Add the cooked noodles, chicken pieces, Worcestershire sauce, salt, pepper, and oregano.
3. Remove from the heat, and pour into a 9 x 13-inch baking dish. Sprinkle with the cheese. Bake until the top is lightly browned, about 45 minutes.

∗ *Makes 6 to 8 servings*

Chicken and Pasta

From the kitchen of D.T.

This recipe has been handed down through three generations. My grandmother used to make this pasta dish. Both my mom and I still make it. It's really delicious. My grandmother used macaroni, my mom uses spaghetti, and I use spinach pasta; but any pasta will do. I have made it so often that I don't use a recipe.

4 tablespoons butter
1½ teaspoons Cajun seasoning
4 boneless, skinless chicken breasts, cut into bite-size pieces
1 large Spanish onion, chopped
1 large green pepper, chopped
1 pound pasta
1 large tomato, diced
1 (4-ounce) can mushrooms, drained and sliced
1 cup black olives, drained and sliced
¾ cup crumbled feta cheese

1. In a medium skillet over medium heat, melt the butter, and sprinkle with Cajun seasonings. Add the chicken to the skillet, and cook until cooked through. Remove from the skillet.
2. In the same skillet, sauté the onion and green pepper until the onion is lightly browned.
3. In a large pot of boiling salted water, cook the pasta until desired doneness. Drain and transfer to a big bowl. Add the diced tomato, mushrooms, black olives, chicken, and sautéed pepper and onions. Mix well, and sprinkle feta cheese throughout the mixture. Serve immediately.

✶ *Makes 4 to 6 servings*

Chicken Parmesan Risotto Casserole

From the kitchen of Robyn Brown

I took my favorite elements of chicken Parmesan and risotto and combined them into one dish.

2 tablespoons olive oil
½ cup diced onion
½ cup sliced mushrooms
4 boneless, skinless chicken breasts
1 (28-ounce) can tomato sauce
1 (10½-ounce) can cream of mushroom soup
½ cup milk
1 teaspoon Italian seasoning
1½ plus ½ teaspoons garlic salt
1 plus 1 cups freshly grated Parmesan cheese
1 cup uncooked rice
1 egg, beaten
1 cup seasoned dried bread crumbs

1. Preheat the oven to 350°.
2. Heat the olive oil in a large skillet over medium heat, and sauté the onion and mushrooms until soft. Remove from the pan.
3. In the same pan over medium heat, sauté the chicken breasts, browning each side for about 1 minute.
4. In a separate bowl, combine the tomato sauce, mushroom soup, milk, Italian seasoning, and the 1½ teaspoons garlic salt. Place 1 cup of this mixture in a separate small bowl.
5. To the larger bowl of liquid mixture, add 1 cup Parmesan cheese, the rice, mushrooms, and onions. Pour into the bottom of a 9 x 13-inch rectangular baking dish. Place the chicken breasts on top of the rice mixture, and cover the chicken with the remaining 1 cup tomato/soup mixture.
6. In a separate small bowl, blend the egg with the bread crumbs, the remaining 1 cup Parmesan cheese, and the remaining ½ teaspoon garlic salt. Mix well. Spread over the top of the casserole.
7. Cover with foil, and bake for 40 minutes. Uncover and continue to bake until the chicken and rice are fully cooked, about 20 more minutes.
8. Serve with additional Parmesan cheese if desired.

✶ *Makes 4 to 6 servings*

1978 Sour Cream Enchiladas

From the kitchen of Pamela Bennett

I was given this recipe by a neighbor when my husband and I were first married and living in Tucson, Arizona. It's an extremely simple recipe and can be made ahead of time. During the first years of our marriage, I liked to prepare this ahead of time so we could just pop it in the oven (no microwave back then) to warm it up when we came home from work. Its mild flavor makes it a long-standing family favorite, even for my daughter, who can't handle spicy foods.

1 (16-ounce) container sour cream
1 (10½-ounce) can cream of chicken soup
4 to 5 boneless, skinless chicken breasts, boiled and shredded
2 to 3 (4-ounce) cans diced green chilies
8 to 10 ounces Cheddar cheese, grated (reserve ⅓ cup for topping)
1 dozen corn tortillas

1. Preheat the oven to 350°. Spray a 9 x 13-inch casserole dish with nonstick cooking spray.
2. Combine the sour cream, soup, chicken, chilies, and grated cheese in a large bowl and mix well.
3. Pour ¼ cup of the mixture into the prepared dish, and spread evenly over the bottom of the dish. Dip 1 tortilla at a time into the chicken mixture in the prepared dish. Spoon 2 to 3 tablespoons of the chicken mixture down the center of the tortilla. Fold the edges across the filling, overlapping slightly. Place seam side down in the casserole dish. Repeat with the remaining tortillas. Top with the reserved ⅓ cup cheese. Bake until bubbly and beginning to brown, about 30 to 45 minutes.

✶ *Makes 6 servings*

Plain Meatloaf

From the kitchen of Elaine Kurschner

Many of my mother's recipes don't have a lot of spices or herbs because my father was allergic to so many of them. Probably as a result, I find that I like plain food sometimes, and this recipe is one I always go back to. To check the seasonings in this meatloaf, I always fry up a little of the meat mixture, taste it, and adjust the seasoning before I bake the whole loaf. My mother loved her meatloaf to have a fine texture, so she mixed the meat very well with her hands, almost mashing it. I like mine a bit coarser, so I am careful not to overmix it.

1 cup dried bread crumbs
3 tablespoons milk
2 pounds ground meat
1 onion, finely minced
¼ cup minced parsley (optional)
1 clove garlic, finely minced
2 eggs
Salt and pepper
1 cup catsup or basic tomato sauce

1. Preheat the oven to 375°.
2. Place the bread crumbs and milk in a large bowl. Stir to blend. Add the meat, onion, parsley, garlic, eggs, and salt and pepper to taste. Mix with your hands until fully combined.
3. In a large baking dish, shape the mixture into a loaf, and bake for 15 minutes. Remove the loaf from the oven, and reduce the heat to 325°. Pour the catsup or tomato sauce evenly over the loaf. Return to the oven, and bake until done, about 1 hour.

✶ *Makes 8 servings*

Corned Beef and Cabbage Casserole

From the kitchen of Marilyn Woods

This is my dear mom's recipe from a long time ago. She never made traditional corned beef and instead used canned, because, having worked her whole life, she always made easy things.

1 small head cabbage, quartered and cored
1 tablespoon oil or bacon drippings
4 green onions with tops, chopped
1 (12-ounce) can corned beef
3 tablespoons butter
3 tablespoons all-purpose flour
1½ cups milk
Salt and pepper
¼ cup dried bread crumbs
1½ tablespoons butter for topping

1. Preheat the oven to 400°. Grease a 1½-quart casserole dish.
2. Cook the cabbage in a large pot of boiling salted water for 20 minutes. Drain.
3. In a skillet over medium heat, heat the bacon grease, and sauté the onions. Add the corned beef, and cook, breaking up the meat and stirring well, for 10 minutes. Remove from the heat.
4. In a heavy saucepan over medium heat, melt the butter, and mix in the flour. Stir in the milk, salt, and pepper. Cook, stirring constantly, until thickened. Remove from the heat.
5. In the prepared casserole dish, layer one-half of the cabbage, one-half of the corned beef, and one-half of the sauce. Repeat the layers. Sprinkle with bread crumbs, and dot with butter. Bake until lightly browned and bubbly, about 30 minutes.

✶ *Makes 6 servings*

Beef Pot Pie

From the kitchen of Elaine Kurschner

1 (10-inch) frozen piecrust with top crust, thawed
1 cup all-purpose flour
½ teaspoon dried thyme, crumbled
1 teaspoon salt
½ teaspoon pepper
2 pounds sirloin, trimmed of all fat and cut in 1-inch pieces
2 tablespoons vegetable oil
1 large onion, chopped
3 carrots, diced
1 rib celery, diced
4 cups beef broth
2 large potatoes, diced
1½ tablespoons all-purpose flour
1 tablespoon butter, softened
2 cups green peas
Salt and pepper
1 egg, lightly beaten with 1 tablespoon water

1. Preheat the oven to 350°. Line a 2-inch-deep casserole dish with the pastry. Weight the pastry with some rice or beans on a piece of foil, and prebake the bottom crust until it is just set, not brown, about 10 minutes. Do *not* bake the top crust.
2. Mix the flour, thyme, salt, and pepper in a paper bag. Add the beef, and shake until all pieces are coated. Dump the meat into a strainer, and shake off the excess flour.
3. In a large, heavy Dutch oven over high heat, heat the vegetable oil. Working in batches, brown the beef until it is all browned. With a slotted spoon, transfer the meat to a platter, and pour off some of the fat from the pot. Add the onions to the pot, and cook until they soften. Add the carrots and celery, and continue cooking until the onions are brown. Return the meat to the pot.
4. Add the beef broth, and reduce the heat to low. Cover and cook for one hour. Add the potatoes, and cook until they are tender, about 30 to 45 minutes. If necessary, add more broth.
5. Blend the flour and soft butter together in a small bowl until they form a smooth paste. Add the paste in bits to the stew, stirring well after each addition, until the sauce is thick. Stir in the peas. Remove from the heat and taste. Adjust the seasoning with salt and pepper to taste. Set aside, and allow to cool. Can be done ahead. Preheat the oven to 425°.
6. Spoon the stew into the crust. Dampen the edges of the crust with the beaten egg. Lay the top crust over the entire casserole. Gently press the edges to seal. Brush the top of the crust with the beaten egg. Using a small knife, cut slits in the top crust. Bake until brown and juices are bubbling, about 40 minutes.

✶ *Makes 6 servings*

College Time Pot Roast

From the kitchen of Cindi Klein

Our family has enjoyed this pot roast for years. Our children in college love it because it's made in one pan and is easy and delicious. There are usually leftovers.

2¼ pounds beef brisket
2 carrots, chopped in large chunks
2 ribs celery, chopped in chunks
1 onion, chopped coarsely
1 (14-ounce) can stewed tomatoes
2 tablespoons firmly packed brown sugar
Large dash of salt and pepper

1. Preheat the oven to 350°.
2. Take four large pieces of aluminum foil, and lay them in a cross pattern. Place the brisket fat side up in the center of the foil. Stack the carrots, celery, onion, and tomatoes on top of the meat, with the tomatoes on top. Sprinkle with brown sugar, salt, and pepper. Wrap the meat and vegetables very tightly with the foil, and place it in an aluminum pan. Set the pan in the oven. Bake for approximately 2 hours at 350°. Lower the oven temperature to 250° and cook for 1 more hour. Lower the oven temperature again to 225° and cook for 1 final hour. (Cook for a total of 4 hours.)
3. Remove the pan from the oven and let sit, unopened for 15 minutes. To serve, unwrap the roast on a serving dish. The meat will have made its own sauce. Allow to cool slightly. Cut the meat in thin slices against the grain. Serve with baked potatoes or noodles.

✶ *Makes 8 to 12 servings*

Red Wine Pot Roast

From the kitchen of Robin Falck

One of my favorites recipes is this pot roast. It was my birthday dinner for many years. We have taken to calling it "Burnt Pot Roast," though. My mom was browning the pot roast one day when a friend of hers stopped by. I happened through the kitchen while they were in the living room talking and noticed that the pot with the meat in it was on fire. From the kitchen door, I called, "The roast is burning!" Mom replied, "Oh, yeah, it always does that." So, I grabbed the pot off the stove, carried it to the doorway, and asked, "Like this?"

For the marinade:

1 cup red wine
1 cup water
2 large onions, sliced
1 lemon, sliced
2 tablespoons sugar
1 tablespoon salt
1 teaspoon ginger (optional)
12 whole black peppercorns

For the roast:

3 to 4 pounds lean beef roast
2 plus 2 tablespoons fat
2 tablespoons flour

1. To make the marinade, combine the wine, water, onions, lemon, sugar, salt, ginger, and peppercorns in a large bowl. Set the roast in a shallow glass or ceramic baking dish, and pour the marinade over it. Cover with plastic wrap, and set in the refrigerator to marinate up to 24 hours.
2. To cook the roast, remove the meat from the marinade. Over medium-high heat, put 2 tablespoons of the fat in a deep pot. Add the meat to the pot, and brown it on all sides. Strain the marinade, and add it to the pot. Cover and simmer 3 to 4 hours. Remove the meat from the pot, and allow it to rest briefly. Reserve the marinade and cooking liquid in the pot.
3. Meanwhile, in a small sauté pan over medium-high heat, melt the remaining 2 tablespoons fat. Stir in the flour, and cook, whisking constantly, for 5 minutes. Add the mixture to the marinade, and cook, stirring constantly, until slightly thickened to make a gravy. Return the meat to the pot with the gravy in it, and heat 5 minutes more. Serve with wide, flat noodles and a salad.

✶ *Makes 8 to 10 servings*

Hungarian Goulash

From the kitchen of Elaine Kurschner

1¼ pounds stew beef, cut into 1-inch pieces
1¼ pounds pork, cut into 1-inch pieces
Salt and pepper
2 tablespoons vegetable oil
1¼ pounds onions, chopped
1 large green bell pepper, chopped
1 large red bell pepper, chopped
2 cloves garlic, minced
4 tablespoons sweet paprika
2 (15-ounce) cans crushed tomatoes
2 cups water
2 tablespoons cornstarch dissolved in 2 tablespoons water

1. Season the meat with salt and pepper. In a large pot over high heat, add the oil and, working in batches, brown the meat. Transfer each batch to a separate plate. Add the onions and peppers to the pot, and sauté until the onions are soft and translucent.
2. Return all the browned meat to the pot, and add the garlic and paprika. Continue to cook until the garlic is soft. Add the tomatoes and water. Bring the mixture to a boil and reduce the heat. Simmer about 45 minutes. If the mixture is too thin, add the cornstarch, and bring the sauce to a boil for an additional 3 minutes, stirring constantly.

✶ *Makes 6 to 8 servings*

Mom's Beef Stew

From the kitchen of K.P.

My cousin and I both make this stew the same way. I thought it was just my mother's recipe, but clearly my grandmother taught both my aunt and mother to make it the same way. Sometimes I add mushrooms or even zucchini when they're in season. Cooking this in a slow cooker makes it a snap, but if you don't have one, a heavy pot on the stove will do. Perfect for a cold and rainy day.

2 pounds stew beef, cut into bite-size pieces
1 (10¾–ounce) can tomato soup
2 large carrots, peeled and cut into 3-inch pieces
3 large potatoes, peeled and chunked
1 medium onion, diced
1 rib celery, diced
1 teaspoon Lawry's seasoned salt
½ teaspoon garlic pepper
1 teaspoon Worcestershire sauce
1 whole bay leaf

1. In a slow cooker, combine the meat, soup, carrots, potatoes, onion, celery, seasoned salt, garlic pepper, Worcestershire, and bay leaf. Turn the temperature on low, and allow the mixture to cook at least 8 hours.
2. To cook on the stove, place the meat, soup, carrots, potatoes, onion, celery, seasoned salt, garlic pepper, Worcestershire, and bay leaf in a large, heavy pot and combine well. Turn the heat on low, cover, and cook, stirring occasionally, until the meat is cooked through and vegetables are tender, about 5 hours.

✶ *Makes 6 servings*

Braised Pork

From the kitchen of Jenney T.

I often call my mom to get a recipe that I remember from childhood. I'll say, "I feel like having such-and-such. I remember you made it once." My mom's dishes are really simple. They only require a few ingredients. She was a career mom, so she didn't have a lot of time for cooking. This is one of my favorites.

2 tablespoons oil
1 pound pork tenderloin, sliced into ¼-inch-thick rounds
1 bunch scallions, chopped into 1-inch-long pieces
1 tablespoon chopped chili pepper
4 tablespoons soy sauce

1. Heat the oil in a Dutch oven or other large pot. Add the pork to the pot, and cook until browned on all sides. Add the scallions, pepper, and soy sauce to the pot. Add enough water to barely cover the meat. Bring the water to a boil. Reduce the heat to low.
2. Cover and cook for 30 to 40 minutes or until the pork is cooked through but tender. Serve over rice.

✶ *Makes 4 servings*

Mother's Ham Loaf with Red Currant Sauce

From the kitchen of W.B.

We always had ham around the holidays, and my mom made this ham loaf as a delicious way to use up the leftovers.

For the ham loaf:

1 pound ground ham
¾ pound ground pork
1 cup soft fresh bread crumbs
⅓ cup chopped onion
1 egg, beaten
½ cup milk

For the sauce:

½ cup red currant jelly
1½ teaspoons grated orange peel
2 tablespoons orange juice
1 tablespoon prepared horseradish

1. Preheat the oven to 350°.
2. Combine the ham, pork, bread crumbs, onion, egg, and milk in a large mixing bowl. Mix thoroughly. In a shallow baking dish, shape the mixture into a loaf. Bake until done, about 1¼ hours. Remove from the oven, and let rest for 5 minutes.
3. Meanwhile, prepare the currant sauce. In a medium saucepan over low heat, mix the jelly, orange peel, orange juice, and horseradish. Cook, stirring constantly, until the sauce is smooth and hot.
4. Spoon some of the sauce over the cooked ham loaf, and serve the remaining sauce on the side.

∗ *Makes 8 servings*

Ham and Pea Salad

From the kitchen of Sherry Knackstept

I got this recipe a long time ago from a friend of mine. It's a great way to use up your Easter leftovers.

2 cups cooked, diced ham
1 (10-ounce) package frozen peas, cooked
2 eggs, hard cooked, cooled, and diced
¼ cup chopped sweet pickles
1 tablespoon grated onion
¼ cup diced green pepper
¾ cup mayonnaise

1. Combine the ham, peas, eggs, pickles, onion, green pepper, and mayonnaise in a large bowl. Mix well. Cover and refrigerate for at least 2 hours.

✶ *Makes 6 servings*

Kapusta (Pork and Cabbage Stew)

From the kitchen of Trina Cieply

This is the way my grandmother made Kapusta, which technically means "cabbage" or a "cabbage dish," and I still make it like this. Some traditional variations don't use meat at all, while others substitute lamb or smoked sausage for the pork. I have often used leftover pork or lamb to make this. If you need more water during cooking, just add some. The resulting dish should have some liquid but not be soupy.

1 plus 1 tablespoons cooking oil
4 pork chops, whole or diced into bite-size pieces
2 onions, sliced
2 cloves garlic, minced
1 large cabbage, cored and roughly chopped (or 2 bags slaw mix)
1 (26-ounce) can stewed tomatoes, with juice
1 large carrot, shredded
2 tablespoons brown sugar
1 cup tomato juice or water

1. Heat 1 tablespoon oil in a skillet over medium-high heat, and add the meat. Cook until browned on both sides. Drain the fat, transfer the meat to a plate, and reserve.
2. In a large pot over medium-high heat, heat the remaining 1 tablespoon oil, and sauté the onions. Add the garlic, cabbage, and tomatoes, breaking the tomatoes apart with your hands as you add them. Stir in the carrot, meat, and brown sugar. Add the tomato juice. Bring to a boil, reduce the heat, cover, and simmer until the cabbage is soft, at least 1 hour.

✶ *Makes 6 servings*

Pork Adobo

From the kitchen of Tamara Rivera

My husband's father learned to prepare this dish when he was in the navy and stationed in the Philippines. When I serve this, inevitably, there is a fight over who gets to eat the wonderful, flavor-soaked garlic. So, in an effort to preserve the peace, I usually add many more cloves of garlic. You can easily substitute chicken for the pork.

4 to 6 pork chops or 2 pounds pork loin sliced 1 inch thick
1 cup soy sauce
⅔ cup white vinegar
3 to 5 whole cloves garlic, peeled
1 bay leaf, crumbled

1. Place the pork in a large skillet or Dutch oven over high heat. Cover with the soy sauce and vinegar. Add the garlic and bay leaf. Bring the mixture to a boil, and then reduce the heat to allow the liquid to simmer.
2. Cover and cook, turning every 30 minutes, until the meat is very tender, about 2 hours. Serve over steamed rice.

✶ *Makes 4 to 6 servings*

Lolah Lazo's Adobo

From the kitchen of Alysia Korelc

Being half Filipino, I had the pleasure of enjoying many traditional Filipino dishes at gatherings with relatives and family friends. Everyone seemed to have his or her own versions of various dishes, but we always liked Mom's or Grandpa's the most. Mom made her adobo with pork or chicken, while one of my grandfathers made his with venison. The very first thing Mom always told us before starting any recipe was, "Put on a pot of rice." So, whatever meat you choose to use, first put on a pot of rice.

2 pounds pork, cut into bite-size cubes
½ cup white or apple cider vinegar
2 cups water
2 cloves garlic, minced
Soy sauce
Salt and pepper

1. In a deep skillet or large saucepan over high heat, combine the pork, vinegar, water, and garlic. Bring this to a boil, and then reduce the heat.
2. Cover the pot and simmer, stirring occasionally, until the liquid evaporates and the pork is tender, about 40 to 50 minutes. Season with the soy sauce, salt, and pepper to taste. Serve with hot, steamed rice.

Variations: Instead of pork, use 2 pounds boneless, skinless chicken breasts or venison. You may need to add more water to cook the venison until tender.

∗ *Makes 8 servings*

City "Chicken"

From the kitchen of Lee Ann Burgess

After September 11, I was ready for things to start returning to as close to normal as possible. I realized our lives had changed forever, but I also knew it was important to go on with the things we enjoyed prior to the tragedy. This old, beloved, family recipe is one of those things. The name of this recipe comes from the trick I pulled on my family the first time I made it: None of them likes pork, and they were all convinced this was chicken.

½ cup all-purpose flour
½ teaspoon garlic powder
¼ teaspoon pepper
¼ teaspoon salt
2 pounds boneless pork, cut into cubes
4 tablespoons butter
1 envelope onion soup mix
1 (14½-ounce) can chicken broth
1 cup water

1. In a shallow bowl, combine the flour, garlic powder, pepper, and salt. Toss the pork cubes in the flour mixture to coat.
2. Melt the butter in a large frying pan over medium-high heat, and add the pork cubes. Sauté, stirring, until browned evenly. Drain the excess butter. Sprinkle the soup mix over the pork, and add the broth and water. Reduce the heat, cover, and simmer until tender, about 1 hour. Remove the cubes from the sauce. Continue to cook the sauce until it is thickened. Serve the sauce over mashed potatoes along with the pork.

✶ *Makes 4 servings*

Heirloom Rice and Sausages

From the kitchen of M.R.

My grandma used to make this rice dish. My kids love it, but my husband won't go near it.

2 cups uncooked rice
2 cups frozen peas
4 cups water or chicken stock
1 tablespoon olive oil
1 pound Italian sausage links
2 cloves garlic, crushed
1 medium onion, finely chopped

1. Combine the rice, peas, and water or stock in a medium saucepan over medium-high heat. Bring to a boil, cover, and reduce heat. Cook until all the liquid is absorbed. Remove from heat.
2. Meanwhile, in a large, deep skillet over medium heat, heat the oil, and sauté the sausages. Cook until done, and with a slotted spoon, transfer to paper towels to cool slightly. Transfer to a board, and carefully cut the sausages into ½-inch-thick slices.
3. To the same skillet, add the garlic and onion, and sauté until soft, but do not brown. Return the sliced sausages to the skillet, and sauté briefly. Remove from the heat, and add the cooked rice. Stir well to coat the rice. Serve immediately.

✶ *Makes 6 servings*

Italian Sausage with Peppers

From the kitchen of Elaine Kurschner

Here's my favorite do-ahead crowd pleaser. Make this several days in advance, refrigerate, and reheat the day of the party. Great in a slow cooker.

5 pounds Italian sausage, hot, sweet, or combination, cut into 3-inch pieces
5 cups chopped green bell pepper
2 cups chopped onion
6 cloves garlic, chopped
8 to 10 cups canned, diced tomatoes with juice

1. Working in batches, in a skillet over high heat, sauté the sausage until browned and cooked through. Transfer the browned sausages to a large pot.
2. When all the sausages are cooked, pour off the fat and reduce the heat to low. To the same skillet, add the green peppers and onions, and sauté until soft and translucent, scraping up the browned bits from the bottom of the pan. Add the peppers and onions to the large pot with the sausages, and place over medium-high heat. Stir in the garlic and tomatoes, cover, and simmer for 1 hour. Serve with crisp Italian bread or rolls.

✶ *Makes 10 to 12 servings*

BBQ Kielbasa and Beans

From the kitchen of M.R.

Prepared in a slow cooker or in the oven, these Polish sausages are terrific.

2 pounds turkey kielbasa, cut into ½-inch slices
2 (15-ounce) cans Great Northern Beans, drained and rinsed
1 (28-ounce) can crushed tomatoes
½ large Spanish onion, chopped
½ cup molasses
½ cup brown sugar
2 cloves garlic, crushed

1. Preheat the oven to 350°. Grease a 3-quart casserole dish.
2. Mix the kielbasa, beans, tomatoes, onion, molasses, brown sugar, and garlic in a large bowl. Pour into the prepared dish. Cover and cook for 1 hour.

✶ *Makes 6 servings*

Bratwurst

From the kitchen of G.W.

For this recipe it is essential to use Samuel Smith Oatmeal Stout. I cannot stress this enough. We've tried other stouts, but they turn bitter and make this totally inedible. With the right beer, though, these turn out just delicious served with potato hoagie rolls, grated sharp Cheddar, and sandwich stacker dills.

2 packages of Johnsonville bratwurst (this is the best we've found)
2 (12-ounce) bottles Samuel Smith Oatmeal Stout
2 tablespoons butter
1 green bell pepper, sliced into thin strips
1 red bell pepper, sliced into thin strips
2 medium white onions, sliced into thin strips
Salt and pepper
1 to 2 cups sauerkraut
¼ cup water

1. Place the bratwurst and stout in a cast iron skillet over medium heat. Bring to a boil, and reduce the heat to a simmer. Cook, stirring occasionally, until the stout reduces to a syrupy glaze. Be careful not to overcook because the glaze will burn.
2. Meanwhile in a small pan over medium heat, melt the butter and sauté the peppers and onions until soft and translucent. Mix in the salt and pepper to taste.
3. When the bratwurst is done, remove from the pan. To the same pan, add the sauerkraut and water. Cook until the liquid has evaporated. Serve the sauerkraut alongside the bratwurst.

✶ *Makes 6 servings*

Pizza Loaf

From the kitchen of Caryn Dubelko

My mom has made this for Super Bowl Sunday for as long as I can remember. She said the recipe originally came from my grandma. It is so good, I don't know why we didn't have it more often. It's similar to a calzone, but with a taste all its own. Enjoy!

1 loaf frozen bread dough
1 pound freshly ground sausage (Italian style is best)
1 medium onion, diced
1 (6-ounce) can tomato paste
½ teaspoon dried oregano
¼ teaspoon kosher salt
¼ teaspoon pepper
¼ teaspoon garlic salt
1 cup pepperoni slices
1 cup diced green peppers
1 cup sliced mushrooms
½ cup grated Parmesan cheese
½ cup melted butter
1 cup shredded mild Cheddar cheese
1 cup shredded mozzarella cheese

1. Thaw the dough, and let it rise to double the size.
2. Cook the sausage and onions in a large skillet over medium heat until the meat is browned and the onions translucent. Drain the fat from the pan.
3. In a large bowl, mix the sausage and onions together with the tomato paste, oregano, salt and pepper, garlic salt, pepperoni, green peppers, mushrooms, and Parmesan cheese. If the mixture is too thick, add a few tablespoons of water to thin it out to a spreadable consistency.
4.  Preheat the oven to 350°.
5. Punch down the dough on a floured surface, and roll it out into a ¼-inch-thick oval. (*Note:* If the dough springs back while rolling out, allow it to sit for 15 minutes to "relax," and then proceed with rolling again.) Brush the dough with the melted butter. Place the dough on an ungreased cookie sheet. Spoon the filling down the center of the length of the dough in a 2- to 3-inch line, leaving 1 to 2 inches of uncovered dough at the top and the bottom. Top with the Cheddar and mozzarella cheeses.
6. Bring the edges of the long sides of the dough oval together over the filling, and pinch to seal along the entire length of the dough. Using a sharp paring knife, cut several small slits in the dough along both sides of the seam to allow the steam to escape. Bake for 30 minutes or until the crust is golden brown and the cheese is melted.
7. Allow the baked loaf to cool for at least 10 minutes before slicing with a bread knife to serve.

✶ *Makes 6 to 8 servings*

Cod with Tomatoes and Peppers

From the kitchen of Elaine Kurschner

This is a very old recipe from my grandmother. It's almost fat free, because you use just enough olive oil to coat the pan—about one tablespoon.

1 tablespoon olive oil
1 medium onion, chopped
1 green bell pepper, cut in 1-inch pieces
1 clove garlic, minced
1 (28-ounce) can stewed tomatoes
2 pounds cod fillets, cut in 3-inch pieces
4 fresh basil leaves
Salt and pepper

1. In a heavy saucepan, heat the oil and sauté the onion, pepper, and garlic until soft, about 5 minutes. Add the tomatoes, and bring to a boil. Reduce to a simmer. Place the pieces of cod on the tomatoes, cover, and simmer until the fish flakes easily, about 20 minutes.
2. Tear the basil leaves into the pot just before serving, and season with the salt and pepper to taste. Serve with lots of bread.

✶ *Makes 6 servings*

Salmon Patties

From the kitchen of M.G.

My husband was raised eating these salmon patties, so I make them for him and my boys. I used my mother-in-law's recipe until I decided to adjust it a bit to make the patties more moist. The guys love them.

2 (6-ounce) cans boneless, skinless salmon
18 saltine crackers, ground
½ to 1 teaspoon celery seed
1 egg, lightly beaten
½ to ¾ cup mayonnaise
Freshly ground black pepper
1 drop Tabasco (optional)
18 saltine crackers, crushed
2 to 4 tablespoons butter

1. In a large bowl, combine the salmon, ground saltines, celery seed, egg, mayonnaise, pepper, and Tabasco. Mix gently until a dough is formed. Mold into four to six patties. Place the crushed saltines in a shallow bowl, and coat the patties with the saltines.
2. Melt the butter in a large skillet over medium-high heat. Add the patties, and fry, adding additional butter to the skillet if needed, until they are browned on both sides and crusty.

* *Makes 4 to 6 servings*

Jason's Grilled Garlic Shrimp

From the kitchen of Stacia Jesner

My husband, by and large, doesn't cook unless it involves an open flame. This is one of his tried and true grill recipes. He made it up one afternoon when he had bought shrimp for dinner but had neglected to get any other ingredients. We always have garlic and olive oil on hand, and I keep a rosemary plant in the kitchen window. (Don't try this with dried rosemary; it's too crunchy.) It's great to make with kids. They have a lot of fun putting the shrimp on the skewers.

6 (6-inch) wooden skewers
24 large shrimp, peeled and deveined, tails left on
4 cloves garlic, crushed and peeled
Leaves from 3 large sprigs of rosemary
½ cup olive oil

1. Soak the skewers in a bowl of water for at least 30 minutes so that they do not burn on the grill. Thread the shrimp onto skewers, four per skewer. Place the skewered shrimp in a small baking dish.
2. In the bowl of a food processor, chop the garlic and rosemary leaves until fine. Add the oil and pulse to blend. (Garlic and rosemary may be chopped by hand and whisked into the oil in a bowl.) Pour the marinade over the shrimp. Cover and refrigerate for about 30 minutes.
3. Heat the grill to medium-high heat. Place the skewered shrimp on the grill. Cook for 2 to 3 minutes on each side.

✶ *Makes 4 servings as an appetizer, 2 as a main course*

Mom's Tuna Casserole

From the kitchen of Stacia Jesner

My mother always made this as Friday night dinner during Lent. It's one of my favorite comfort foods, and my mom knows this. She brought a big dish of it to my house right after my first baby was born.

1 cup uncooked elbow macaroni
2 (6-ounce) cans tuna fish, drained and flaked
1 rib celery, chopped fine
1 small yellow onion, chopped fine
1 cup water
1 (10½-ounce) can cream of mushroom soup
½ cup plain dried bread crumbs
2 tablespoons butter, cut into small pieces

1. Preheat the oven to 400°. Grease a small baking dish.
2. Cook the macaroni according to package directions. Drain and cool.
3. In a large bowl, combine the macaroni, tuna fish, celery, onion, water, and cream of mushroom soup. Mix well. Pour into the prepared dish. Evenly spread the bread crumbs over the top of the mixture. Dot with the butter, and bake until bubbly, about 50 minutes.

✶ *Makes 4 servings*

Shrimp Gumbo

From the kitchen of G.W.

My family loves a good pot of gumbo, and this is one of the best recipes my husband and I have found. We started with a Cajun recipe and then added some "tweaking" of our own. It takes two days to make and costs a bit as well, but the final flavors are worth every minute and every penny.

3 pounds shrimp, uncooked with heads and shells on
1 large onion, quartered, plus 2 cups chopped onion
4 ribs celery with tops, coarsely chopped, plus 2 ribs celery, chopped
2 plus 2 whole bay leaves
1 bunch parsley, stems and leaves, chopped
¼ plus ½ teaspoon thyme
1 plus 4 tablespoons vegetable oil
2 tablespoons white vinegar
2 tablespoons seafood seasoning
2 tablespoons salt
2 tablespoons plus ½ teaspoon cayenne
2 tablespoons plus 1 teaspoon liquid crab boil (Zatarain's brand is best)
4 tablespoons all-purpose flour
½ cup chopped bell pepper
½ cup sliced Polish or Andouille sausage
6 cloves garlic, minced
2 quarts chicken stock
4 cups strong brewed coffee
1 pint oysters with liquid or 2 (6-ounce) cans undrained crabmeat
1 large bag frozen sliced okra

1. Rinse the shrimp under cold water, and place in the bottom of a large stockpot. Cover with the 1 large onion, the 4 ribs celery, 2 bay leaves, the chopped parsley, the ¼ teaspoon thyme, 1 tablespoon oil, the vinegar, seafood seasoning, salt, 2 tablespoons cayenne, and 2 tablespoons crab boil. Mix well and cover tightly. Place over medium-high heat, and cook without removing the cover for exactly 5 minutes.
2. Uncover the pot, and stir the shrimp from bottom to top. Cover and cook 5 minutes longer. Stir again. The shrimp liquid should be boiling. Cover and cook until the shrimp are pink, about 2 minutes longer. Do *not* overcook. Remove from the heat, and let the shrimp rest 3 minutes to absorb the seasonings.
3. Peel and devein the shrimp without rinsing. Do this over the pot so you won't lose any "shrimp butter," and set the shrimp aside. With a slotted spoon, transfer the vegetables to a sieve placed over a bowl. Press out the juices from the vegetables with the back of a spoon, and add the juices back to the large stockpot. Discard the vegetables.

4. Place the same stockpot over medium-high heat, and add the flour. Sauté, stirring constantly, until the flour is dark brown and smells nutty, about 3 to 5 minutes. Add the remaining 4 tablespoons oil, the remaining 2 cups chopped onion, the bell pepper, and the remaining 2 ribs chopped celery. Cook until the vegetables are softened. Add the sausage and garlic, and sauté. Add the chicken stock, coffee, the remaining 2 bay leaves, the remaining ½ teaspoon thyme, the remaining ½ teaspoon cayenne, and the remaining 1 teaspoon crab boil. Stir well, and add the oysters (or crabmeat). Bring to a boil, and reduce the heat to a simmer. Cook for at least 3 hours, stirring occasionally. Add additional brewed coffee or chicken stock if the mixture gets too dry. Do *not* add water. Remove from the heat, and allow to cool. Cover and refrigerate 8 to 10 hours.
5. Return the stockpot to medium heat, and bring the mixture to a simmer. Add the okra. Allow to simmer for 3 to 6 hours.
6. Just before serving, add the cooked shrimp, and cook until just heated or the shrimp will toughen. Serve over a bowl of rice, sprinkle with gumbo filé, and serve with a big loaf of French bread.

✶ *Makes 10 servings*

Shrimp in Tomatoes and Feta

From the kitchen of Stacia Jesner

A hand-me-down from a friend of mine, the original recipe listed "1 pound shrimp, 1 stick butter, 1 head of garlic, 1 pinch cayenne pepper." Although I've toned it down a bit and rounded out the flavors with the tomato and feta cheese, you still might want to have breath mints handy after dinner. This is a good "last minute company" Saturday night dinner. It never fails to please, and many of those who have eaten it ask me to make it the next time they plan to come over.

4 tablespoons butter
4 tablespoons olive oil
4 cloves garlic, finely chopped
1 pound shrimp, peeled and deveined
1 (28-ounce) can diced or chopped tomatoes
1 bay leaf
1/4 teaspoon paprika
1/8 teaspoon cayenne
4 ounces feta cheese, cut into small cubes

1 Melt the butter and oil in a heavy skillet over medium-high heat. Add the garlic, and sauté for 1 minute. Add the shrimp, and sauté for about 3 minutes. Add the tomatoes, bay leaf, paprika, and cayenne, and stir well to mix. Cook for about 10 minutes. Stir in the feta cubes. Cover and cook until cheese begins to melt, about 5 to 10 minutes more.

 Serve with rice and crusty bread to soak up the sauce.

* *Makes 4 servings*

4

Pasta, Rice, and Potatoes

Aunt Mary's Pasta

From the kitchen of Elaine Kurschner

This recipe is measured by how many eggs you use. It's two large eggs to each cup of flour. So when my Aunt Mary would make a batch, she would say "I made four eggs' worth of pasta." This recipe can be used to make straight, long noodles, but it also works well for different shapes. Wide lasagna noodles are easy to cut and so are smaller squares and triangles that are great cooked in soup.

2 cups all-purpose flour	**4 large eggs**

1. On a board or flat surface, make a mound of flour with a well in the center. Break the eggs into the well, and beat with a fork, gradually incorporating the flour into the egg. Mix until a soft, elastic dough forms. It may require more or less flour depending on the size of the eggs. The dough should hold together and be easy to handle.
2. Remove any stray pieces of dough from the board, and lightly flour. Knead the dough by folding it over on itself and pressing down with both hands for at least 10 minutes. Form into a ball, and place in a bowl. Cover with a towel, and let the dough rest for about 1½ hours.
3. Divide the dough into thirds, and place one piece on a lightly floured surface. For long noodles, roll the dough into a rectangle the length you want your noodles to be. Let the dough rest until the surface dries out slightly, about 10 minutes. Starting at the short side, gently roll the dough into a jelly roll. Cut across the roll at 1-inch intervals, making pinwheels. Unroll into long strands, shake off any excess flour, and allow to dry slightly before cooking. The dough can be frozen at this point.
4. In a large pot of boiling salted water, cook the noodles until al dente, about 30 to 60 seconds.

✶ *Makes 2 to 4 servings*

Grandma's Egg Noodles

From the kitchen of Vicki McCandless

My grandma made these noodles regularly, always using sifted flour and blending them by hand. Like pie crust, the secret to tender noodles is not overmixing. My grandma's noodles were delicious, and when I was little, I got to help with pulling the noodles apart. After the noodles dry, they freeze well placed in a plastic bag.

3 egg yolks
1 whole egg
3 tablespoons water
1 teaspoon salt
2 cups sifted flour

1. In a small bowl, beat the egg yolks and whole egg until light. Whisk in the water and salt. In a separate large bowl, place the flour in a mound, making a well in the center. Pour the egg mixture into the center of the mound, and stir until just combined. Divide the dough into thirds.
2. Transfer the dough to a lightly floured surface. With a rolling pin, roll out each part as thin as possible (paper thin). Let rest about 15 minutes. Using a very sharp knife, cut into thin strips. Pull the noodles apart, shake off excess flour, and lay out to dry.
3. To cook, bring a large pot of broth or water to a rolling boil. Add the noodles and cook until tender, about 5 minutes.

✶ *Makes 6 to 8 servings*

Homemade Manicotti

From the kitchen of Giovanna Roy

My mom's friend, whose family grew up in Naples, gave my mother this recipe for the crepes, and we just used the filling that we normally use for our ravioli. It does take a little time to make the crepes, but it is so well worth it. Don't be afraid to be a little aggressive with the seasonings. I've noticed that ricotta tends to be bland sometimes.

For the crepes:

1 cup all-purpose flour
4 eggs
1 tablespoon olive oil
1 teaspoon salt
1 cup water

For the ricotta filling:

1 pound ricotta cheese
2 eggs
½ cup chopped flat leaf parsley
1 cup Parmesan cheese
Salt and pepper
4 cups shredded mozzarella cheese
4 to 6 cups tomato sauce (recipe follows)

1. Preheat the oven to 350°.
2. To make the crepes, combine the flour, eggs, olive oil, salt, and water in a medium bowl. Stir until smooth.
3. Heat a small skillet over medium-high heat, and lightly brush it with olive oil. Ladle enough batter into the pan to cover the bottom. Cook until the top is set and the bottom is slightly golden, about 30 seconds. Transfer the crepe to wax or parchment paper, and repeat the cooking process until all the batter is used, stirring well before pouring each crepe. Allow to cool.
4. To make the filling, blend the ricotta, eggs, parsley, Parmesan cheese, and salt and pepper to taste in a medium bowl.
5. To assemble, sprinkle a little mozzarella down the middle of each crepe, and spoon 2 or 3 tablespoons of the ricotta filling in a line down the center of each crepe. Fold the edges to create rolls. Spoon a thick layer of tomato sauce into a 9 x 12-inch baking pan. Place the rolls, seam sides down, in the pan. Rolls should fit snugly, but not too tight. Use an additional 8 x 8-inch pan for the leftover rolls. Cover the manicotti generously with sauce, and sprinkle with the remaining mozzarella cheese.
6. Cover with foil, and bake until bubbly, about 45 minutes to 1 hour.

✶ *Makes 6 to 8 servings*

Basic Tomato Sauce

From the kitchen of Giovanna Roy

3 tablespoons olive oil
2 medium onions, chopped
2 to 3 cloves garlic, minced
1 to 1½ pounds ground beef
2 Italian sausages, hot or sweet, chopped
Salt and pepper
1 (28-ounce) can whole tomatoes in juice
2 (28-ounce) cans crushed tomatoes
1 to 2 teaspoons sugar (optional)
¼ cup chopped fresh basil

1. Heat the olive oil in a large, heavy saucepan over low heat, and slowly sauté the onions, stirring often. Cook until they are soft and translucent. Add the garlic, and cook until the onions are beginning to brown slightly, about 5 minutes. Do not allow the garlic to brown.
2. Add the ground beef, sausage, and salt and pepper to taste to the saucepan. Increase the heat, and brown the meat until it is no longer pink. When the meat is done, tilt the pan and pour off about three-fourths of the fat from the bottom of the pan. Add the whole and crushed tomatoes, salt and pepper to taste, sugar, and basil.
3. Reduce the heat and simmer for 1 to 2 hours. Serve with any kind of pasta.

✶ *Makes 1½ quarts sauce (enough for a 9 x 13-inch lasagna or manicotti)*

Spinach Lasagna

From the kitchen of M.P.

Even my kids like this. It's one of my favorite ways to get them to eat their spinach.

1 pound lean ground beef
2 (14-ounce) cans Italian stewed tomatoes
2 (8-ounce) cans tomato sauce
2 (14-ounce) cans whole-leaf spinach, well drained
1 pound package ricotta cheese
9 lasagna noodles (1 package), cooked according to package directions and drained
3 cups shredded mozzarella cheese
¼ cup Parmesan cheese

1. Preheat the oven to 350°.
2. Brown the meat in a large skillet over medium-high heat. Add the stewed tomatoes and tomato sauce, and cook for 5 minutes.
3. Place the spinach in a strainer, and squeeze out any excess water. Combine the spinach and ricotta in a small bowl. Mix well.
4. Spoon 3 to 4 tablespoons of the tomato mixture into a 9 x 13-inch baking dish. Spread it evenly over the bottom of the pan. Lay three of the noodles on top of the sauce. Scatter half the spinach mixture over the noodles, spoon one-third of the remaining sauce over the spinach, and sprinkle one-third of the mozzarella over the sauce. Repeat the layers, ending with the mozzarella. Top with Parmesan cheese, and bake until bubbly, about 30 minutes. Serve with extra Parmesan cheese.

✶ *Makes 6 to 8 servings*

Spaghetti and Meatballs

From the kitchen of Elaine Kurschner

At our house these are referred to as "black meatballs" and I always (as my mother and grandmother did) set some on one side to be served just as they are. These can be frozen on a cookie sheet, then put into a plastic bag to store. You will notice that I don't put garlic into my meatballs—it's just our family recipe, but if you want garlic, add some.

For the basic tomato sauce:
- **6 tablespoons olive oil**
- **1 cup finely chopped onion**
- **2 cloves garlic, cut in half**
- **4 cups peeled, seeded, and diced fresh tomatoes with juices**
- **1 cup canned tomato purée**
- **¼ cup tomato paste**
- **Salt**
- **¼ to ¾ cup red wine**

For the meatballs:
- **1 egg, beaten**
- **¼ cup milk**
- **1½ cups fresh bread crumbs**
- **½ pound ground beef**
- **½ pound ground pork**
- **½ pound ground veal**
- **¼ cup chopped fresh parsley**
- **½ cup very finely chopped onion**
- **4 tablespoons grated Locatelli or Romano cheese**
- **Salt and pepper**
- **4 tablespoons olive oil**

For the spaghetti:
- **1½ pounds dried spaghetti**

1. To make the sauce, heat the olive oil in a large pan over medium heat. Add the onion, and sauté until soft, about 5 to 8 minutes. Add the garlic, and sauté until the garlic is soft, about 3 minutes. With a slotted spoon, remove the garlic from the pan, and discard. Add the fresh tomatoes with their juices, canned tomato purée, tomato paste, salt to taste, and ¼ cup red wine. Mix well. Bring to a boil, and reduce to a slow simmer. Cover and cook for 30 minutes, stirring often. If the sauce becomes too thick, add more red wine, bringing the mixture to a boil each time you add wine to boil off the alcohol.
2. To make the meatballs, beat the eggs and milk together in a large bowl. Add the bread crumbs, and let soak until the liquid is absorbed, about 3 minutes. Add the meats, parsley, onion, cheese, and salt and pepper to taste. Using your hands or a wooden spoon, mix well.
3. In a large skillet, heat the olive oil. Sauté 1 tablespoon of the meat mixture until crisp. Remove the skillet from the heat. Taste the small meatball, and adjust the

seasonings for the whole mixture accordingly. Form the meat mixture into balls. Return the skillet to the heat, and sauté the meatballs until dark brown, about 15 minutes. Using a slotted spoon, transfer the cooked meatballs to a plate. Drain the fat from the pan, and return to the heat. Add 1 cup of the cooked sauce to the pan to deglaze the pan, scraping up all the scraps of meat. Transfer the sauce with the scrapings back to the large pot of sauce, rinse the skillet with 2 to 3 tablespoons red wine, and add that to the pot. Add the reserved meatballs, and mix well. Cover and simmer the sauce for 15 minutes.

4. Meanwhile, bring a large pot of salted water to a boil. Add the spaghetti, and cook until al dente, about 5 to 6 minutes. Drain and serve with the meatballs and sauce.

✶ *Makes 8 servings*

Linguine with Clam Sauce

From the kitchen of Giovanna Roy

My mom used to make this for dinner once a week, and we never got tired of it. It tastes great and is fast to make, too. I have no idea where the bread crumbs came in, but I know my Nana used to do the same thing. It must be some kind of Sicilian thing.

¼ cup extra virgin olive oil
2 cloves garlic, minced
⅓ cup chopped fresh, flat leaf Italian parsley
2 (6½-ounce) cans chopped or minced clams with juice
1 (14-ounce) bottle clam juice
Salt and pepper
1½ cups fresh Italian bread crumbs
2 to 3 tablespoons olive oil
1 pound linguine

1. Heat the oil in a small saucepan over medium heat. Add the garlic, and cook just slightly, about 1 to 2 minutes. Do not let it brown. Add the parsley, stir to coat it with the oil, and cook 1 to 2 minutes.
2. Add the clams with their juice and the bottle of clam juice to the saucepan with the parsley and garlic. Bring the mixture to a boil, add the salt and pepper to taste, and let simmer.
3. In a separate, small skillet over medium-low heat, sauté the bread crumbs with just enough olive oil to moisten the crumbs. Cook, stirring constantly, until browned. Remove from the heat.
4. Meanwhile, bring the water to a boil, add salt to taste, and cook the linguine until al dente. Drain in a colander, and pour the pasta back into the cooking pot. Add the clam sauce, and toss to mix. Place on a big serving platter, and scatter the toasted bread crumbs on the top.

✶ *Makes 4 servings*

Grandmother's Macaroni and Cheese

From the kitchen of A.M.

This is the best recipe for mac and cheese, and it's my grandmother's.

1 (8-ounce) box elbow macaroni
2 pounds medium Cheddar cheese, shredded
2 eggs, beaten
3 (5-ounce) cans evaporated milk
1 tablespoon butter
Salt and white pepper

1. Preheat the oven to 350°. Lightly grease a 9 x 13-inch baking dish.
2. Bring a large pot of salted water to a boil over high heat. Add the macaroni, and cook until just tender, about 6 minutes. Do not overcook. Drain in a colander, and allow macaroni to cool briefly.
3. Transfer to a large bowl, and add the cheese, eggs, milk, butter, and salt and pepper to taste.
4. Pour the macaroni mixture into the prepared dish. Cover with foil, and bake in the middle of the oven until bubbly, about 45 minutes.

✶ *Makes 6 servings*

Amish Macaroni Salad

From the kitchen of Sherry Knackstept

Many of my friends and family members are Amish and Mennonite, and one of them gave me this recipe. It's a bona fide heirloom. I've heard so many people say that their grandmothers fixed salad the same way.

1 pint Kraft Miracle Whip salad dressing
¼ cup vinegar
¾ cup sugar
2 tablespoons prepared mustard
1 (16-ounce) box elbow macaroni or shells, cooked as directed and drained
½ cup chopped celery
½ cup finely grated carrots
¼ cup finely chopped onions
5 plus 1 hard-cooked eggs, sliced
Paprika

1. Blend the Miracle Whip, vinegar, sugar, and mustard in a small bowl. Mix well. In a large mixing bowl, combine the macaroni, celery, carrots, onions, and 5 sliced eggs. Reserve 1 sliced egg for garnish. Mix gently. Add the dressing, and mix gently again. Garnish with paprika and the reserved sliced egg.

✶ *Makes 10 to 12 servings*

Lolah Lazo's Pancit

From the kitchen of Alysia Korelc

My mother, also known to her grandchildren as Lolah Lazo, made pancit (pronounced "pahn-sit") for just about every special family occasion while we were growing up, and it's always the first dish we request even now. My mom's family and part of my father's family were from the Philippines. So we were raised with plenty of Filipino "soul food." Although we've had pancit made by other people at parties or picnics over the years, there is nothing like Mom's. This recipe was passed down from her mother. Now I'm teaching my own daughter how to make it.

1 pound Chinese flat noodles or linguine
3 tablespoons vegetable oil
1 teaspoon sesame oil
1 clove garlic, minced
1 small onion, minced
1 cup diced pork
1 cup medium shrimp, shelled, deveined, and patted dry
1 (14-ounce) can chicken broth
¼ pound Chinese pea pods (optional)
2 medium carrots, cut julienne-style (optional)
Salt or fish sauce
Black pepper
¼ cup diced scallions
4 hard-cooked eggs, sliced
1 to 2 lemons, cut into 8 wedges

1. Boil the noodles according to package directions. Meanwhile, in a deep skillet or large pot, sauté the garlic and onion in hot vegetable oil and sesame oil until the onion is soft and translucent. Add the diced pork, and sauté until tender and browned. Remove from the pan with a slotted spoon.
2. In the same pan, sauté the shrimp until pink. Add the chicken broth, pea pods, carrots, and cooked pork. Lower the heat, and simmer for 5 minutes. Add the salt or fish sauce and black pepper to taste. Add the drained noodles, toss, and mix well. Transfer to a serving platter. There should be some pan juices to pour over the noodles.
3. For the garnish, sprinkle the diced scallions over the pancit, then arrange the sliced egg on top. Arrange the lemon wedges around the edge of the platter.

Variation: You can substitute 2 boneless, skinless chicken breasts, boiled and shredded, for the pork and shrimp.

✶ *Makes 6 servings*

Pierogies

From the kitchen of Belinda Naismith

Pierogies (or piroshki, as they are also called) are part of the traditional Ukrainian Christmas Eve meal. I learned how to make them from my mother, who learned from her mother, who learned from my great-grandmother. I look forward to teaching my own daughter to make them.

For the pierogies:
8 cups flour
¼ teaspoon salt
1½ teaspoons baking powder
1 cup margarine, melted
3 cups hot water

For the filling:
2 cups cottage cheese OR
2 cups mashed potatoes mixed with sautéed onions

For the garnish:
8 tablespoons butter
2 small onions, chopped

1. Combine flour, salt, and baking powder in a large bowl. Stir in the margarine and water to create a dough. Cover and let sit for 2 to 6 hours. Roll out the dough to ¼-inch thickness.
2. Cut the dough into circles, using the bottom of a drinking glass or a 3-inch biscuit cutter. Re-roll scraps as needed.
3. Place 1 tablespoon of the selected filling in the center of the circle, and fold the dough over the filling. Pinch the edges to close to prevent the circles from opening. Line a tray with a cloth or wax paper. Repeat the process, and lay the pierogies on the tray, separating the layers with wax paper as you go.
4. Bring a large pot of salted water to a boil. Working in batches of about six at a time, drop the pierogies one by one into the water. Cook the pierogies until they float, about 3 to 4 minutes. Remove from the boiling water with a slotted spoon. (The pierogies may be frozen at this point. Thoroughly defrost before proceeding with the next step.)
5. To serve, melt the butter in a sauté pan. Add the onions and boiled pierogies, and cook, stirring lightly, until the onions are translucent and the pierogies are lightly browned.

✶ *Makes 6 to 7 dozen pierogies*

Spinach Rice Dish

From the kitchen of Ginny Pigott

This is my mother-in-law's recipe, and it's terrific.

1 (10-ounce) package frozen chopped spinach, thawed and drained
1 cup cooked rice
⅓ cup milk
1 egg, beaten
½ cup grated Cheddar cheese
½ teaspoon dried thyme
1 teaspoon Worcestershire sauce
1 (5-ounce) can water chestnuts (optional)

1. Preheat the oven to 350°.
2. In a large bowl, combine the spinach, rice, milk, egg, cheese, thyme, Worcestershire, and water chestnuts. Mix well.
3. Pour the mixture into a glass pie pan. Bake for 1 hour.

✶ *Makes 4 to 6 servings*

Baked Rice Fluff

From the kitchen of C.M.

Ever since I was a kid, this has been one of my favorite side dishes. It goes especially well with Easter dinner.

3 eggs, separated
1 small onion, halved
½ cup butter, melted
1 cup cubed Cheddar cheese
1 cup parsley sprigs
2 cups cooked rice

1. Preheat the oven to 350°. Grease a 2-quart casserole dish.
2. Working in the bowl of a food processor or blender, place the egg yolks, onion, butter, and cheese, and process until smooth. Add the parsley, and process only enough to chop. Transfer to a large bowl, and combine with the cooked rice. Mix thoroughly.
3. In a large bowl, beat the egg whites until stiff. Fold gently into the rice mixture.
4. Pour the combined mixture into the prepared dish, and bake until heated through and lightly browned, about 25 minutes.

✶ *Makes 8 servings*

Wild Rice with Pecans and Mushrooms

From the kitchen of Ginny Pigott

I've enjoyed this wonderful dish at my mother-in-law's house many, many times.

½ pound wild rice
3 cups water
1½ teaspoons salt
1½ cups sliced mushrooms
½ cup butter
Freshly ground black pepper (optional)
½ cup coarsely broken toasted pecans
Chopped parsley for garnish

1. Soak the rice in water for 8 to 10 hours. Drain, wash well, and put in a medium saucepan. Cover with the water, add the salt, and bring to a boil. Reduce the heat to low, cover, and cook until tender, about 1 hour. If necessary, drain the excess water. Transfer to a large bowl.
2. In a skillet, melt the butter and sauté the mushrooms until wilted and tender. Add the pepper, and transfer to the bowl with the rice. Add the pecans and toss. Serve garnished with parsley.

✶ *Makes 8 to 10 servings*

German Potato Pancakes

From the kitchen of Marilyn Woods

My grandmother served the most delicious potato pancakes, with good homemade applesauce. My grandmother, however, did not give me this recipe. She always cooked "by guess and by golly" and never had any need to write down a recipe. So this is my reconstruction of the recipe, using the ingredients I remember that she used. I always overindulged when she made them, and these are very close to hers. In fact, I'm hungry for them right now.

5 to 6 medium potatoes, peeled and coarsely grated
½ medium onion, coarsely grated
1 egg
6 tablespoons milk
½ teaspoon salt
⅛ teaspoon pepper
3 to 6 tablespoons all-purpose flour
Vegetable oil for frying

1. In a medium bowl, combine the grated potatoes, onion, egg, milk, salt, and pepper. Mix well, and gradually stir in the flour until all the moisture is absorbed.
2. Heat 2 tablespoons oil until it is hot but not smoking. Working in batches, add large spoonfuls of potato mixture to the oil, flattening them with a metal spatula into pancake shapes. Fry until browned, about 3 to 4 minutes. Turn and cook until the other side is browned and crisp. With a slotted spoon, transfer the cooked pancakes to a plate lined with paper towels. Serve immediately or keep warm on a baking sheet in a 200° oven until the entire batch is done. Repeat until all batter is used.
3. Serve with butter and applesauce.

✶ *Makes 6 servings*

Creamed Potatoes

From the kitchen of Susan Cabral

These are the best and easiest potatoes I have ever had, and they go very well with a salty dish like ham.

1 to 2 pounds new potatoes, peeled and sliced ⅛ inch thick
Salt and pepper
1 to 2 cups heavy cream

1. Preheat the oven to 350°.
2. Rinse the potatoes, and place them in a large bowl. Cover with heavily salted water, and soak for at least 30 minutes. Drain the potatoes, and discard the water.
3. Place the potatoes in 9 x 13-inch casserole dish. Add salt and pepper to taste. Pour the heavy cream over the potatoes, covering three-fourths of the way up the potatoes. Bake until the cream is bubbly and the tops of the potatoes are slightly browned and tender, about 45 minutes to 1 hour.

✶ *Makes 6 to 8 servings*

My Mom's Stuffed Potatoes

From the kitchen of I.F.

In honor of the 21st anniversary of my mom's death and what should have been her 87th birthday, I offer this dish of hers, which has a funny story attached to it. Mom always worried about her chicks who had "left the nest." When she invited us for dinner, she always cooked more than we needed and sent it home with us.

One Sunday she outdid herself. She prepared a stuffed Cornish hen for each of us, an artichoke stuffed with ground beef and bread crumbs, and this stuffed potato recipe. Wow! What a meal that was. Needless to say, we took home plenty of stuff. We always appreciated her cooking. Now, whenever I make these, I say, "Thanks, Mom, for the great memories and for taking such good care of us."

6 large Idaho potatoes, scrubbed
4 tablespoons butter
½ cup milk
Salt and pepper
2 eggs, separated and lightly beaten
1 cup chopped ham

1. Preheat the oven to 400°.
2. Score the potatoes, and bake them on a rack in the center of the oven until tender, about 1 hour. Remove from the oven, and allow them to cool slightly. Carefully, slice the top one-third off each potato. With a spoon, carefully scoop out the insides of both the tops and bottoms of the potatoes, and transfer them to a large bowl. Reserve the bottom (larger) portion of the potato skins, discarding the top one-third of each. With a fork or potato masher, mash and blend with the butter and milk and salt and pepper to taste. Transfer 1 cup of the mashed potatoes to a separate small bowl.
3. Add the lightly beaten egg whites and ham to the large bowl of mashed potatoes. Mix well. Add the egg yolks to the small bowl of mashed potatoes, and blend well.
4. Stuff the reserved potato skins with the ham and potato mixture, topping each potato skin with the egg yolk and potato mixture. Place on a baking sheet, and bake until tops are just beginning to brown, about ½ hour. Serve immediately. Can be frozen.

✶ *Makes 6 servings*

Grandma Rosella's Potato Kugel

From the kitchen of Stacia Jesner

When my husband and I celebrated our first Passover together, his grandmother sent me a packet of her special holiday recipes. Each one was written out in loving "old lady scrawl," which she hoped I could read. (I could, but a few confirmation phone calls to Florida were required.) Having her specialties on the table for our seder creates a connection between generations. I especially like this kugel; it comes out like a giant, baked potato pancake. I always claim the crispy edges.

2 pounds potatoes, peeled
1 medium onion
1 large carrot
¼ cup matzo meal
2 eggs
1 teaspoon salt
⅛ teaspoon pepper
3 tablespoons chicken fat (available in little containers from butcher stores near Passover)

1. Preheat the oven to 350°. Grease a 9 x 9-inch baking dish.
2. Grate the potatoes, onion, and carrot. In a large mixing bowl, combine the grated vegetables with the matzo meal, eggs, salt, and pepper. Stir in the chicken fat and mix well.
3. Transfer the potato mixture to prepared dish, spreading it evenly over the dish. Bake uncovered until lightly brown all over and the edges are crisp, about 90 minutes.

✶ *Makes 6 servings*

German Potato Salad

From the kitchen of J.B.

My husband is German, and in his hometown an Annual Heritage Fest is held each summer. The main foods served at the fest are German Potato Salad and Bratwurst. German Potato Salad is a nice change of pace and very easy to make.

½ pound of bacon, diced small
1 gallon potatoes, cooked, peeled, and sliced
3 tablespoons bacon grease
1 small onion, diced
2 cups water
1 cup vinegar
1 scant cup sugar
3 tablespoons cornstarch dissolved in 3 tablespoons water
Salt and pepper

1. Sauté the bacon in a skillet over high heat until brown. With a slotted spoon, transfer the bacon to a medium bowl with the sliced potatoes.
2. To the same skillet, leaving the bacon grease, add the onion, water, vinegar, and sugar. Bring to a boil, and cook for 1 minute. Stir in the dissolved cornstarch, and cook for 3 to 5 minutes longer. Season with salt and pepper to taste. Pour the warm sauce over the potatoes, and mix gently. Serve warm.

✶ *Makes 8 to 10 servings*

Aunt Sallie's Hot Potato Salad

From the kitchen of Elaine Kurschner

When I went to a covered-dish supper one Friday night, I had the most wonderful hot potato salad. I tracked down the person who brought it, and she got the recipe from her late great-aunt, who made it for every family occasion. What I liked about it was the real potato taste, not drowned in a lot of strong dressing. Her big secret is that she bakes the potatoes.

6 or 8 medium red potatoes
1 tablespoon butter
1 egg, beaten
¼ cup sugar
¼ cup cider vinegar
1 tablespoon cornstarch
1 teaspoon dry mustard
1 teaspoon celery seeds
Dash of red pepper
Salt and pepper
¼ cup heavy cream
1 small red onion, finely minced
1 cup diced celery
4 hard-cooked eggs, chopped
2 tablespoons minced fresh parsley
6 sweet gherkin pickles, minced
Paprika
Minced fresh parsley for garnish

1. Preheat the oven to 400°.
2. Prick the potatoes with a fork several times, and rub the butter over the skins. Place in the oven directly on the oven rack. Bake until tender but not overcooked, about 40 minutes. Allow to cool for 10 minutes.
3. Meanwhile, with an electric mixer, beat together the egg, sugar, vinegar, cornstarch, mustard, celery seeds, and red pepper. Transfer to a small saucepan over medium-high heat, and cook, stirring with a wooden spoon, until thick. Add the salt and pepper to taste. Stir in the cream. Cook for 1 minute. If the mixture is too thick, add more cream until the dressing is a little thinner than mayonnaise. Remove from the heat.
4. Dice the hot potatoes with their skins into 1-inch cubes. In a large mixing bowl, place the diced potatoes, onion, celery, eggs, parsley, and pickles. Add the warm dressing, and toss gently, being careful not to break up the potatoes and eggs. When well mixed, top with the paprika and parsley.
5. Serve hot. May be reheated in the oven or microwave.

Note: To double the recipe, it is best to mix in two batches.

∗ *Makes 6 to 8 servings*

Mom's Potato Salad

From the kitchen of L.L.

My family loves this potato salad for picnics because it is colorful and has a wonderful tang. The secret is in the potato preparation. The recipe came from my mom, who got it from her mother. I put the eggs on top, because my husband won't eat hard-cooked eggs, and he can work around them this way.

5 to 6 medium white or new potatoes, peeled and quartered
2 to 3 tablespoons white vinegar
Salt and pepper
2 tablespoons chopped dill pickles
¼ cup chopped celery
2 tablespoons chopped green onion
2 tablespoons grated carrot
2 tablespoons chopped green pepper
1 cup mayonnaise
2 hard-cooked eggs, sliced, optional (for garnish)

1. In a medium pot of boiling water over high heat, cook the potatoes until just fork tender. Do *not* overcook the potatoes. Drain and coarsely dice.
2. Place the potatoes in a glass or ceramic mixing bowl, toss with the vinegar, and generously sprinkle with the salt and pepper to taste. Set aside to cool.
3. Add the pickles, celery, onion, carrot, green pepper, and mayonnaise to the cooled potatoes. Toss gently. Cover and refrigerate 8 to 10 hours or until well chilled.
4. Arrange the egg slices in a circle around the top of the potato salad.

✶ *Makes 6 servings*

5

Soups, Sides, and Salads

Chinese Watercress and Meatball Soup

From the kitchen of J.T.

As a child, this was my favorite soup. When I started to talk, I couldn't quite pronounce the word for "watercress" in Chinese, so I called it "little veggie soup." I still do sometimes.

For the broth:

1 quart water or chicken broth
1 bunch watercress, washed very well and cut into 2-inch segments
1 carrot, cut into ⅛-inch discs

For the meatballs:

¼ pound ground pork
1 tablespoon cornstarch
2 to 3 teaspoons sesame seed oil, or to taste
2 tablespoons water
Salt and pepper

1. To prepare the broth, in a 2-quart saucepan over high heat, bring the water (or broth) to a boil. Add the watercress and carrots. Return the broth to a boil. Reduce the heat to low, and allow the broth to simmer.
2. To prepare the meatballs, in a medium mixing bowl, combine the pork, cornstarch, oil, water, and salt and pepper to taste. The water and cornstarch will make the meatballs lighter and fluffier. Form ½-inch meatballs.
3. To finish the soup, raise the heat to high, and bring the broth back to a boil. Drop the meatballs into the boiling broth, and cook for about 10 minutes. Serve immediately.

* *Makes 2 servings*

Mom's Matzo Ball Soup

From the kitchen of Betty Cohen

On Passover, I'm usually making many other dishes, and I'm short on preparation time because I work full-time. So, after several years of trying to make my own matzo ball soup from scratch, using a chicken, I decided I needed a shortcut. I took my mother's recipe and simplified it, but I kept the chicken fat in the matzo balls rather than using a healthier alternative like vegetable oil, because, for one reason, it really adds a nice flavor. And, two, I felt better doing it my mother's way.

For the matzo balls:

2 tablespoons melted chicken fat
2 eggs, slightly beaten
½ cup matzo meal
1 teaspoon salt
Dash of white pepper
1 tablespoon chopped parsley
1 to 2 tablespoons chicken broth
4 quarts water or canned chicken broth

For the soup:

2 (48-ounce) cans chicken broth
½ onion, chopped
2 ribs celery with leaves
3 to 4 sprigs fresh parsley
3 to 4 sprigs fresh dill
2 chopped carrots
Salt and pepper

1. To make the matzo balls, in a large mixing bowl, lightly mix together the chicken fat and eggs with a fork. Add the matzo meal, salt, pepper, and parsley to the chicken fat/egg mixture. Add the 1 to 2 tablespoons broth, and stir to form a batter. Refrigerate for 30 minutes. Using wet hands, form the batter into balls, slightly smaller than the size of a golf ball.
2. In a large stockpot over high heat, bring the water (or broth) to a boil. Drop the matzo balls into the boiling liquid. Reduce the heat to low, and simmer, partially covered, for 30 minutes. Remove the matzo balls from the cooking liquid with a slotted spoon. Set aside the matzo balls, and discard the cooking liquid.
3. To make the soup, in a large stockpot over high heat, combine the canned chicken broth, onion, celery, parsley, dill, and carrots. Bring the mixture to a boil, and let it simmer for 1 hour, partially covered. Add the salt and pepper to taste.
4. To serve, place one matzo ball in each of eight individual soup bowls. Ladle the soup over each matzo ball.

✶ *Makes 8 servings*

Mom's Beef-Vegetable Soup

From the kitchen of Stacia Jesner

I always think of this as "Halloween Soup." When we were kids, my mom would make a huge pot of this soup and serve it with a crusty loaf of bread for a simple, quick supper before we headed out for trick-or-treating. (In those days, kids still got to go out after dark, and on their own). Whenever I make this soup now, it brings back that amazing feeling of anticipation and excitement of Halloween night.

6 to 8 beef short ribs
3 tablespoons vegetable oil
2 quarts water
1 onion, coarsely chopped
1 rib celery, left whole
2 carrots, cut into 1-inch chunks
1 (28-ounce) can whole plum tomatoes, with liquid
2 ribs celery, cut into 1-inch chunks
2 beef bouillon cubes
2 bay leaves
1 teaspoon chopped fresh garlic
1 teaspoon dried thyme
1 (10-ounce) package frozen peas or 1 (10-ounce) package frozen green beans

1. In a large stockpot over medium-high heat, brown the short ribs in the vegetable oil. When brown on all sides, add the water, onion, whole celery rib, and the carrots. Reduce the heat to low. Cook, partially covered, for 30 minutes. Remove the celery rib with tongs or a slotted spoon.
2. Add the canned tomatoes with their liquid to the pot. Break up the tomatoes by pressing them against the side of pot with a wooden spoon. Add the celery pieces, bouillon cubes, bay leaves, garlic, and thyme. Cook, partially covered, for 1½ to 2 hours. Remove the pot from the heat.
3. Remove the short ribs from the pot using a slotted spoon or tongs. Allow them to cool. With your fingers, pull the meat from the bones, discarding any fat or gristle. Shred the meat and return it to the pot. Discard the bones, fat, and gristle.
4. Place the pot, covered, in the refrigerator for 8 to 10 hours, or overnight, to allow the fat from the meat to rise to the top and congeal. Before serving, skim the hardened layer of fat from the top of the soup. Add the frozen peas or green beans, reheat for 30 minutes, and serve.

Variation: Add ½ cup uncooked barley or wild rice to the soup for the last 30 minutes of cooking.

∗ *Makes 8 to 10 servings*

Mom's Speedy Chicken Noodle Soup

From the kitchen of Betty Cohen

I made up this recipe over the years, using my mother's theory of cooking, which never had exact measurements. She used to always say, "I don't know what I do; I just kind of do it. Throw in a little of this, a little of that, and you're done." It works pretty well.

2 (48-ounce) cans chicken broth
½ onion, chopped
2 ribs celery with leaves
3 to 4 sprigs fresh parsley
3 to 4 sprigs fresh dill
2 carrots, chopped
3 to 4 chicken thighs
4 to 8 ounces fine or broad noodles
Salt and pepper

1. In a large stockpot over high heat, combine the chicken broth, onion, celery, parsley, dill, carrots, and chicken thighs. Bring the mixture to a boil, and reduce the heat to low. Simmer for 1 to 1½ hours, partially covered. Add the noodles, and continue to simmer for an additional 15 to 20 minutes. Add the salt and pepper to taste.

∗ *Makes 8 servings*

Cheese Soups

Editor's note: These three versions of cheese soup all use Velveeta—the favorite American processed cheese that was introduced by Kraft in 1928. But this American kitchen standard was foreign to one of our British community members, who couldn't wait to try this soup and had never heard of Velveeta. Unfortunately, these recipes will have to remain American heirlooms, since there is no British equivalent for Velveeta.

1886 Cheese Soup

From the kitchen of A.M.

It is a tradition at our house to serve this delicious soup on Christmas Eve. It is even better if made the day before serving.

¼ cup butter
½ cup minced onion
½ cup finely chopped celery
½ cup finely grated carrots
½ teaspoon garlic powder
½ teaspoon paprika
2 teaspoons all-purpose flour
4¼ cups chicken broth
2 cups whole milk
2 cups heavy cream
1 pound Velveeta cheese, cubed
Handful of dried or fresh parsley
Salt and pepper

1. In a 4-quart pot over medium-low heat, melt the butter, and sauté the onions, celery, and carrots until tender.
2. In a separate medium bowl, combine the garlic powder, paprika, and flour, and blend thoroughly. Whisk just enough chicken broth into the flour to make a thick paste.
3. Add the remaining broth to the pot with the vegetables, and bring to a boil over medium heat. Whisk in the flour/broth mixture, and stir well. Reduce the heat to low, and add the milk, cream, cubed cheese, and parsley. Continue to cook for 10 to 15 minutes. Season with the salt and pepper to taste. Serve with a crusty loaf of French bread.

∗ *Makes 6 to 8 servings*

Cheese and Potato Soup

From the kitchen of H.A.

3 cups diced potatoes
1 cup sliced celery
1 cup peeled and diced carrots
1 large sweet onion, diced
3 cups water
2 tablespoons butter
2 tablespoons flour
2 cups milk, hot
1 pound Velveeta cheese, cubed
1 (10-ounce) can cream-style corn
Freshly ground pepper

1. In a large saucepan or Dutch oven over medium-low heat, combine the potatoes, celery, carrots, onion, and water. Bring to a boil, and cook until the potatoes are tender, about 20 minutes.
2. In a small saucepan over medium heat, combine the melted butter and flour. Stirring constantly, cook for 2 minutes to create a white roux. Slowly add the hot milk, stirring constantly. Cook for 3 more minutes.
3. When the potatoes are tender, stir in the cubed cheese, and cook for 1 minute. Add the corn and milk sauce, stirring well until heated through. Season with freshly ground pepper to taste.

⁎ *Makes 6 servings*

Cheesy Potato Soup

From the kitchen of C.M.

My five-year-old and my husband absolutely love this soup. It's so easy to make and so flavorful.

3 fresh potatoes, peeled and cubed
2 cups water
4 tablespoons butter
1 onion, chopped
3 carrots, peeled and grated
3 ribs celery, chopped
2 (10½-ounce) cans chicken broth
2 (10½-ounce) cans potato soup
1 (4-ounce) can chopped green chilies
1 pound Velveeta cheese, cubed
1 cup sour cream

1. Cook the potatoes with about 2 cups water in a large saucepan over medium-high heat. Cook until just tender, about 5 to 10 minutes. Remove from the heat and drain. Reserve the potatoes, and return the saucepan to the stove.
2. In the same saucepan over medium heat, melt the butter, and add the onions, carrots, and celery. Sauté until the onions are soft and translucent. Add the chicken broth, soup, potatoes, and chilies. Simmer for ½ hour. Add the Velveeta, and simmer until melted, stirring constantly. Mix in the sour cream. Remove from the heat and serve.

✶ *Makes 4 to 6 servings*

Lentil Soup

From the kitchen of Giovanna Roy

I just love this hearty soup. We ate this a lot while I was growing up, and I never got tired of it. Feel free to add anything you want, like more veggies or even more broth, since it's a pretty thick soup. It makes a great lunch or light supper entrée.

3 tablespoons olive oil
3 ribs celery, sliced
3 carrots, sliced
2 medium onions, chopped
6 cups chicken broth
1 bay leaf
¼ teaspoon thyme
1½ cups green lentils
2 teaspoons salt
One ham bone or 6 ounces ham steak, cubed (optional)

To serve:
2 cups elbow macaroni pasta, cooked and tossed with olive oil
Parmesan cheese for sprinkling

 In a heavy soup pot over low heat, heat the olive oil, and add the celery, carrots, and onions. Cook until the vegetables are tender (about 10 minutes). Add the broth, bay leaf, thyme, green lentils, and salt. Cook, partially covered, at a simmer for 60 to 90 minutes. If desired, add a ham bone or cubed ham steak for the final 30 minutes of cooking.

2 To serve, ladle the cooked pasta and soup into individual bowls. Sprinkle with the Parmesan cheese.

∗ *Makes 4 to 6 servings*

Grandpa Hubbard's Baked Beans

From the kitchen of S.W.

My grandfather made these beans every weekend in the winter. They were put in the oven with the chicken, meatloaf, ham, or beef roast before leaving for Sunday school and church services. I watched him many times, and even helped when I got old enough, as he "looked over" the dry beans on Saturday evening, washed them, and put them to soak. Even those who normally don't care for baked beans seem to enjoy the taste of these. I have never seen another recipe exactly like this one. And we never knew where my grandfather got this recipe.

My grandfather's original instructions say to put these beans in the oven before church and take them out when you return. My memory is that it took between 2½ and 3 hours, and I have adjusted the recipe accordingly.

This basic recipe makes enough for a small bowl of beans. So if you want some leftovers for baked bean sandwiches, you will need to double it like my grandfather usually did.

1 cup dry Michigan Navy beans, sorted, washed, soaked overnight
2 tablespoons granulated sugar
1 cup firmly packed dark brown sugar
1 small to medium onion, chopped
1 teaspoon salt
Dash of black pepper
2 slices bacon, cut into small pieces

1. Preheat the oven to 325°. Grease a heavy casserole or baking dish.
2. Drain the soaked beans, and place them in a large pot over high heat with 4 quarts fresh water. Do not add salt to the water. Bring to a boil, and cook until tender.
3. Drain the beans, and transfer them to the prepared dish. Add the granulated sugar, brown sugar, onion, salt, and pepper. Mix well. Top with the bacon pieces, and bake for 2½ to 3 hours.

✶ *Makes 2 servings*

My Dad's Baked Beans

From the kitchen of LeeAnn Burgess

My dad gave me this recipe about a year before he passed away. His baked beans were a must at all the picnics—and there were never any leftovers. I have tried many other recipes, but I think this is the best one I have ever had. And to this day, when I make them, I miss my dad.

1 pound bacon
2 (28-ounce) cans Great Northern beans
1 (10-ounce) jar chili sauce
½ cup chopped onion
¼ teaspoon minced garlic
½ cup firmly packed brown sugar
1½ cups molasses

1. Preheat the oven to 400°.
2. Chop half of the bacon into small pieces, and reserve the rest in long slices. In a large bowl, combine the beans, small bacon pieces, chili sauce, onion, garlic, brown sugar, and molasses. Mix well. Pour into a casserole or roasting pan, and place the remaining slices of bacon on top. Bake, uncovered, until the bacon is crispy and the sauce has thickened, about 1 hour.

✶ *Makes 6 to 8 servings*

Pinto Beans with Salt Pork

From the kitchen of D.N.

This recipe has been handed down in my family from generation to generation, and my children make it as well. We always covered the soaking beans with a tea towel. I think my grandmother did that because there weren't any screens on her windows, and she wanted to keep the bugs out. But I actually don't know the reason; I simply know that I was taught to do it and so I still do.

The modern microwave instructions are all my own. I was a high school vocal music director for 21 years, and once while with my vocal ensemble on a singing tour, we rented a beach house. I forgot to put the beans out to soak for our supper, but I remembered that my home economics teachers taught us to get bread dough to rise quickly in the microwave. I thought to use the same method to hurry the beans to soak. The rest, as they say, "is history."

I always serve this with cornbread. Depending on how much water I add while I am cooking the beans, the cornbread serves to soak up the extra liquid. My son-in-law loves these beans served with fried salt pork, hot cornbread with butter, pan-fried potatoes, sliced tomatoes and onions, and fried okra.

1 pound dried pinto beans
4 to 6 slices salt pork, cut into pieces
Salt

1. Wash the beans, pick over them, and discard any rocks and bad beans. Place the beans in a large colander, and rinse them with cold water until the water runs clear, about 3 or 4 times. Place in a large bowl, and cover with water. Place a tea towel over the bowl, and soak overnight.
2. After soaking, drain the beans, and place in a large pot over high heat. Add 4 quarts water or enough water to generously cover the beans. Stir in the salt pork, but do *not* add additional salt. Bring to a hard boil, and then reduce the heat to a medium boil. Cover and cook until the beans are very soft, about 1 to 2 hours. Taste and, if necessary, add salt, and cook 5 minutes more.

Microwave soaking instructions: When you forget to soak the beans—or you just come home and decide that evening that you want them—just wash and rinse and place them in a large microwave-proof bowl. Cover with water, and cook in the microwave on high for intervals of 5 minutes, stirring in between each interval. This will cause them to absorb the water. When soaked to your satisfaction, generally about 15 minutes, remove, and put the beans in a cooking pot. Continue cooking according to the instructions above.

✶ *Makes 6 to 8 servings*

Grandma Edwards's Oyster Dressing

From the kitchen of Maribeth Pittman

My father's mother, Myrtle Goldie Musick Edwards, was a legendary cook. Most of her delicious offerings were Indiana-farmwife-homey: sweet chunky applesauce, rich egg noodles, and fruit pies with delicate, flaky crusts. Oyster dressing was her single foray into the "exotic," and it was made only for our big family Christmas dinners. Midwestern landlubbers that we are, this is one seafood dish that my family embraces as a tradition.

1 pint fresh shucked oysters with their liquid
2 cups medium-coarse Ritz cracker crumbs
½ cup butter, melted
Freshly ground black pepper
¾ cup half-and-half
½ teaspoon salt
¼ teaspoon Worcestershire sauce
Fresh lemon juice

1. Preheat the oven to 350°. Grease an 8-inch square baking dish.
2. Drain the oysters, reserving ¼ cup of the liquid. Pick through the oysters, and remove any shell pieces.
3. In a small bowl, combine the cracker crumbs and butter. Mix well.
4. Spread one-third of the mixture in the bottom of the prepared baking dish. Cover with half the oysters, and sprinkle with the pepper. Cover with another third of the cracker crumbs, the remaining oysters, and a sprinkle of pepper.
5. In a separate small bowl, combine the half-and-half, reserved oyster liquid, salt, Worcestershire sauce, and lemon juice. Mix well.
6. Carefully pour the mixture over the layer of oysters. Top with the remaining cracker crumbs, and bake, uncovered, for about 40 minutes.

∗ *Makes 6 servings*

Ma-Ma's Cornbread Dressing

From the kitchen of A.M.

The signature holiday dish of my maternal grandmother, whom we called "Ma-Ma," was this wonderful cornbread dressing. It is a must on Thanksgiving and Christmas.

2 cups crumbled biscuits (made ahead or store-bought)
4 cups crumbled white cornbread (made ahead or store-bought)
3 to 4 cups chicken or turkey broth
1 onion, finely chopped
1 celery rib, very thinly sliced
1 egg
1 teaspoon dried sage
1 teaspoon baking powder
¼ cup milk

1. Preheat the oven to 450°. Grease a 9 x 13-inch baking dish.
2. Place the biscuits and cornbread in a large bowl, and add 2 cups of the broth. Stir and let stand to soften. Stir in the onion, celery, egg, sage, baking powder, and milk. Stir well, smoothing out all lumps. Stir in more broth until the mixture is the consistency of cornbread batter.
3. Pour into the prepared dish, and bake until set, about 20 minutes. Do *not* overcook.

✶ *Makes 8 to 10 servings*

Asparagus Luncheon Dish

From the kitchen of Giovanna Roy

Salt
2 pounds asparagus, peeled with ends trimmed
4 plus 2 tablespoons butter
4 tablespoons all-purpose flour
1 cup asparagus cooking liquid
1 cup heavy cream
1 to 2 pinches paprika
4 hard-cooked eggs, peeled and sliced
2 cups fresh, soft bread cubes
1 cup coarsely crumbled Ritz crackers
½ cup grated Parmesan cheese

1. Preheat the oven to 350°.
2. Bring a large pot of salted water to a boil over high heat. Cut the asparagus spears into ½-inch pieces. Add the asparagus to the water, and cook 4 to 6 minutes or until soft. With a glass or metal measuring cup, carefully scoop out 1 cup of the cooking liquid and reserve. Drain the asparagus, plunge them into cold water to stop the cooking process, drain well, and reserve.
3. In a saucepan over medium low heat, melt the 4 tablespoons butter. Add the flour, and cook, stirring, for 2 minutes. Whisk in the cup of the reserved cooking water, and then add the cream, stirring until smooth and thick. Cook, stirring constantly, for 8 to 10 minutes. Add the paprika. Season to taste with salt.
4. In a medium baking dish, place one layer of the cooked asparagus, cover with a layer of sliced eggs, and top with half the sauce. Repeat the layering, ending with the sauce on top. Sprinkle with the bread cubes, cracker crumbs, and grated Parmesan cheese. Cut the remaining 2 tablespoons of butter into small pieces, and scatter them over the top of the casserole.
5. Bake until bubbling and golden, about 25 to 30 minutes.

Variation: For a lower fat version, substitute ½ cup chicken broth and ½ cup milk for the 1 cup heavy cream.

✶ *Makes 4 to 6 servings*

Aunt Audrey's Broccoli Casserole

From the kitchen of A.M.

I beg my aunt to make this every year.

4 quarts water
2 (10-ounce) packages frozen, chopped broccoli
1 cup mayonnaise
1 cup Campbell's Cream of Mushroom Soup
1 medium onion, chopped
1 cup grated Cheddar cheese
2 eggs, lightly beaten
1 teaspoon garlic powder
Salt and pepper
1 cup buttered bread cubes (4 slices)
Paprika

1. Preheat the oven to 350°. Butter a 9 x 13-inch casserole dish.
2. In a large saucepan over high heat, bring the water to a boil. Add the broccoli, and cook for 5 minutes. Drain and let stand to cool.
3. Combine the cooled broccoli, mayonnaise, soup, onion, cheese, eggs, garlic powder, and salt and pepper to taste in a medium bowl. Blend well.
4. Pour into the prepared dish, and bake until it is set in the middle, about 30 minutes. Remove from the oven, scatter buttered bread cubes on top, and sprinkle with paprika.
5. Return to the oven, and bake until the bread is golden brown, about 15 minutes. Let stand 10 minutes before serving.

✶ *Makes 8 servings*

Cabbage Pudding

From the kitchen of J.K.

My mother's cousin used to make this recipe for all the family gatherings. I don't make it very often, but I definitely enjoy it when I do.

1 medium cabbage, cleaned
1 tablespoon butter or bacon grease
2 eggs
½ cup milk
18 saltines, crushed
2 dashes freshly ground nutmeg
Salt

1. Remove the 2 or 3 large outer leaves of the cabbage and reserve. Cut the remaining cabbage into large pieces.
2. In a large skillet over medium heat, melt the butter, and add the cabbage pieces. Cover and cook, stirring occasionally, until wilted. Remove from the heat and allow to cool.
3. In a small bowl, combine the eggs, milk, and crackers. Stir in the nutmeg, salt, and wilted cabbage, and mix well. Mold the mixture into a ball, and cover with the reserved outer leaves. Spread a large rectangle of cheesecloth flat on the table or counter. Place the ball in the center. Bring the corners of the cheesecloth together over the top of the ball, and secure together with kitchen twine. Leave several inches of twine to use as a handle.
4. In a large pot over high heat, place enough water to cover half the ball. Bring the water to a boil, and holding the twine handle, lower the ball into the pot. Reduce the heat, and simmer for 30 minutes. Remove from the pot, using tongs or a large slotted spoon. Unwrap the ball from the cheesecloth before serving.

✶ *Makes 8 servings*

Creamy Sauerkraut

From the kitchen of D.L.

My aunt, who is now in her late eighties, still makes sauerkraut the way my grandmother did. She has been writing out some old recipes for me, and this is one I treasure.

1 (28-ounce) can sauerkraut, drained and squeezed dry
2 medium onions, chopped
3 slices bacon, chopped into small pieces
1 tablespoon all-purpose flour
1 large potato, grated

1. In a large skillet over low heat, place the dry sauerkraut, and cover with fresh water. Add half of the chopped onion. Cook for 30 minutes, transfer the mixture to a colander, drain the excess liquid, and return it to the large skillet.
2. In a separate skillet over medium-high heat, sauté the bacon pieces until crisp. Remove from the skillet and reserve. Add the remaining chopped onion to the same skillet, and sauté until tender. Add 1½ cups water to the skillet, and whisk in the flour. Bring to a boil, and add the grated potato. Cook until the sauce thickens, about 10 minutes.
3. Add the thickened sauce to the first skillet with the drained sauerkraut, and return it to medium heat. Mix well, and add the reserved bacon. Cook for 2 minutes and serve.

* *Makes 6 servings*

Fresh Cream-Style Corn

From the kitchen of Elaine Kurschner

I learned how to make this recipe by watching other people do it as I was growing up. In particular, I remember a nifty gadget used by the mother of a college friend of mine: She used a toothed ring that she'd slide down the ear and neatly cut off all the kernels.

Buy or pick the freshest corn you can find. You can purée as much of the corn as you like for the degree of creaminess you want, and no milk or cream is needed.

4 fresh ears corn, shucked and washed
1 tablespoon butter or to taste (optional)
Salt and pepper

1. With a sharp knife score down each row of kernels. Cut the kernels from the cob into a large bowl. Scrape the cob with the back of your knife to extract all the milky juices. Take at least one-fourth of the corn with juice, and purée it in a blender until it is very creamy. Return it to the bowl.
2. Transfer the corn to a saucepan over medium heat, and cook for 5 minutes or until tender. Add the butter, if using, and the salt and pepper to taste.

✶ *Makes 4 servings*

Corn Pudding

From the kitchen of N.D.

1 tablespoon butter, softened for buttering the dish
2 cups corn
2 large eggs, beaten
2 cups milk
1½ tablespoons sugar
½ teaspoon salt
1 tablespoon butter, melted

1. Preheat the oven to 325°. Generously butter a 9 x 13-inch casserole dish.
2. In a large bowl, combine the corn, eggs, milk, sugar, salt, and melted butter. Blend well. Pour the mixture into the prepared dish, and bake until a knife inserted in the center comes out clean, about 30 to 35 minutes.

✶ *Makes 6 servings*

Sweet and Sour Green Beans

From the kitchen of A.B.

At every holiday meal, these green beans are on our table.

1 small onion, diced
4 bacon slices, chopped into pieces
4 tablespoons firmly packed brown sugar
4 tablespoons apple cider vinegar
2 (8-ounce) cans French-style green beans

1. In a medium skillet over medium-high heat, sauté the onion and bacon until the bacon is brown and the onion is soft and translucent. With a slotted spoon, remove the onion and bacon, and drain well on paper towels.
2. In a medium saucepan over medium heat, mix the sugar with vinegar. Add the green beans, cooked onion, and bacon. Cook until heated through and the sugar is dissolved.

∗ *Makes 6 to 8 servings*

Swiss Green Beans

From the kitchen of Marilyn Woods

4 to 5 cups fresh green beans
4 tablespoons butter
4 teaspoons grated onion
½ pound mushrooms, sliced
½ small green pepper, finely chopped
2 tablespoons all-purpose flour
½ teaspoon salt
¼ teaspoon pepper
1 cup sour cream
3 teaspoons sugar
2 cups grated Swiss cheese
1 cup slightly crushed cornflakes

1. Preheat the oven to 350°. Butter a 9 x 13-inch casserole dish.
2. In a large saucepan over high heat, bring 2 quarts of water to a boil. Add the green beans, and cook until crisp and just tender. Transfer to a colander and drain. Run cold water over the beans to stop the cooking process. Drain well and reserve.
3. Melt the butter, and sauté the onion, mushrooms, and green pepper in a large skillet over medium-high heat. Cook until the vegetables begin to soften. Add the flour, salt, and pepper, and cook until thickened. Add the drained beans, sour cream, sugar, and Swiss cheese. Mix well, and remove from heat.
4. Transfer the mixture to the prepared dish, and cover with cornflakes. Bake for 35 to 40 minutes.

✶ *Makes 6 to 8 servings*

Crustless Spinach and Feta Quiche

From the kitchen of Giovanna Roy

My mom got this recipe from a friend she plays bridge with. This would make a perfect dinner for Lent. It's also low in fat and tastes great. The original recipe used one bag of fresh spinach, cleaned, cooked, squeezed dry, and chopped, but a friend of mine—a self-described frugal cook—suggested I try frozen spinach, and the dish turned out great and was much easier.

1 tablespoon dried bread crumbs
1 box frozen, chopped spinach, thawed and squeezed dry
1 cup low-fat ricotta
3 eggs
½ cup half-and-half
⅓ cup feta cheese
¾ teaspoon minced garlic (optional)
½ teaspoon salt
¼ teaspoon pepper

1. Preheat the oven to 350°.
2. Spray a 9-inch pie plate with nonstick cooking spray, and sprinkle with the bread crumbs.
3. In a large bowl, combine the spinach, ricotta, eggs, half-and-half, feta cheese, garlic, salt, and pepper. Beat until fully mixed, and pour into the prepared pie pan. Bake for 35 minutes.

✶ *Makes 6 servings*

Granny's Squash Casserole

From the kitchen of P.N.

Like many old recipes, Granny's recipe only listed the ingredients and left the method for memory. When I make this for myself, I add more squash and use skim milk. My husband found this so delicious and filling that he declared it could be a dinner on its own.

3 cups cubed yellow or green squash
1 medium onion, chopped
5 slices bacon, cooked and cut into small pieces
½ pound Cheddar cheese, grated
4 biscuits, crumbled (made ahead or store-bought)
Salt and pepper
4 eggs
½ cup milk

1. Preheat the oven to 350°. Grease a 9 x 13-inch baking dish.
2. In a large bowl, combine the squash, onion, and bacon. Mix in the cheese, setting aside ⅛ cup cheese for the topping. Mix in the crumbled biscuits, setting aside ⅛ cup for the topping. Mix well, and add the salt and pepper to taste. Transfer the vegetable mixture to the prepared dish.
3. In a separate bowl, combine the eggs and milk. Pour over the vegetables. Top with the reserved cheese and biscuit crumbs.
4. Bake until the squash is soft, about 30 to 45 minutes.

✶ *Makes 6 servings*

Apple and Sweet Potato Casserole

From the kitchen of P.F.

This once-a-year goody has been in my family for three generations. Its unbelievable flavor may make it a favorite in your family as well.

8 to10 large sweet potatoes
4 Granny Smith apples, thinly sliced
¼ cup firmly packed brown sugar
4 tablespoons butter, cut into small pieces
1½ teaspoons cinnamon
1½ teaspoons salt
¾ cup maple syrup

1. Preheat the oven to 400°.
2. Bake the sweet potatoes until just tender, about 40 minutes. Remove from the oven, and set aside to cool. When cool, peel and slice into ½-inch rounds.
3. Reduce the oven heat to 375°.
4. In a large casserole or baking dish, place a layer of potatoes, a layer of apple slices, a sprinkle of brown sugar, a few pieces of butter, a sprinkle of cinnamon, and a pinch of salt. Repeat the layers until the casserole is filled and all the potatoes and apples are used. Pour the maple syrup over the top, and cover with foil. Bake for 1 hour, stirring once. Remove the foil, and bake for 45 minutes longer, stirring occasionally.

✶ *Makes 8 servings*

Zucchini Casserole

From the kitchen of K.M.

You won't believe zucchini could taste so good.

3 quarts water
3 to 4 cups thinly sliced zucchini
2 eggs
1 (16-ounce) can cream-style corn
½ cup shredded Cheddar cheese

1. Preheat the oven to 350°. Butter a 9 x 13-inch casserole dish.
2. In a large saucepan over high heat, bring the water to a boil, and add the zucchini. Cook until just partially cooked, about 2 minutes. Remove from the heat and drain.
3. Beat the eggs in a large mixing bowl. Stir in the corn until thoroughly mixed. Add the zucchini. Transfer the mixture to a prepared dish, and top with the cheese. Bake until a knife inserted in the middle comes out clean, about 1 hour.

Variations: To jazz this up, you can add ¼ cup finely chopped onion, 1 cup whole kernel corn (fresh, canned or frozen), 2 slices crumbled bacon, ¼ cup chopped red or green peppers, or any combination of the above.

✶ *Makes 6 to 8 servings*

Corn, Zucchini, and Tomato Pie

From the kitchen of C.M.

3 cups fresh corn kernels
5 small zucchini, cut into matchstick pieces
1 plus 1 teaspoons salt
½ plus ½ teaspoon black pepper
1 tablespoon chopped fresh dill weed
2 tablespoons melted butter
3 to 4 ripe tomatoes, cut into ½-inch-thick slices
½ cup freshly grated Parmesan cheese
¼ cup dried bread crumbs
2 tablespoons olive oil

1. Preheat the oven to 375°.
2. In a 9 x 13-inch baking dish, combine the corn, zucchini, 1 teaspoon salt, ½ teaspoon pepper, dill, and melted butter. Toss to coat the vegetables. Cover the mixed vegetables with the tomato slices. Sprinkle with the remaining 1 teaspoon salt and ½ teaspoon pepper.
3. In a small bowl, combine the cheese and the bread crumbs. Sprinkle the mixture over the tomatoes, and drizzle with the olive oil. Bake until the edges are bubbly, about 30 minutes. Remove from the oven, and let stand for 5 minutes before serving.

* *Makes 6 to 8 servings*

Egg Salad

From the kitchen of Elaine Kurschner

Egg salad is a personal thing. Whatever we grew up eating is usually how we like it prepared, and everyone's taste is a bit unique, even within families. My mom liked her salad chunky and always diced her eggs. I prefer my egg salad to be spreadable, so I finely chop my eggs. This recipe has consistently worked for both of us.

2 tablespoons minced onion
1 tablespoon mustard
½ cup mayonnaise
6 hard-cooked eggs, diced
½ cup celery, diced
Chopped sweet gherkin pickles, optional
Sliced green olives, optional
Bacon bits, optional
Salt and freshly ground pepper

1. In a small bowl, combine the onion, mustard, and mayonnaise. Blend well.
2. In a separate medium bowl, place the chopped eggs, celery, and any optional additions. Add the mayonnaise mixture and toss. Season with the salt and pepper to taste.

✶ *Makes 6 servings*

California-Style Egg Salad

From the kitchen of C.M.

I got this recipe from one of my sisters-in-law and have since passed this on to as many people as would listen.

4 eggs, hard-cooked, peeled, and chopped
1 avocado, peeled, pit removed, and diced
1 tablespoon chopped onion
1 cup shredded Monterey Jack cheese
1 tablespoon Gulden's spicy deli-style mustard
⅓ cup mayonnaise
Knorr's aromatic seasoning
4 deli rolls
Bean sprouts for garnish

1. Combine the eggs, avocado, onion, and cheese in a medium bowl. Mix in the mustard, mayonnaise, and aromatic seasoning to taste. Stir well.
2. Serve on the deli rolls, and garnish with the sprouts.

✶ *Makes 4 servings*

Bread Salad

From the kitchen of Giovanna Roy

My Nana used to make this recipe, and this is my rendition. She would soak her bread in water, which I thought was disgusting when I was little. Nonetheless, I grew to love this salad despite the squishy bread, which I have transformed into crunchy bread in this version. You can't beat this salad in August when the tomatoes are dead ripe, it's really hot outside, and you don't feel like eating a lot. Make sure you use a good quality Italian bread.

½ large loaf crusty Italian bread
2 tablespoons unsalted butter
1 tablespoon minced garlic
Salt and freshly ground pepper
2 large, vine-ripened tomatoes, diced
⅓ cup chopped fresh basil
½ cup fresh Italian parsley
¼ to ⅓ cup Balsamic Vinaigrette (recipe follows)

1. Preheat the oven to 375°.
2. Using a bread knife with a serrated edge, remove the crusts from the bread. Slice the bread into ¼-inch-thick slices, and then cut it into ¼-inch cubes. You should have about 3 cups of bread cubes total.
3. In a medium skillet over medium heat, melt the butter, and sauté the garlic briefly. Add the bread cubes and salt and pepper to taste. Toss well. Cook briefly until all the bread cubes are coated with butter. Transfer to a baking sheet, and spread evenly in a single tight layer. Use a smaller baking sheet if the cubes are too spread out. Bake, stirring several times, until crisp on the outside but still chewy inside, about 10 minutes. Be careful not to burn. Remove from the oven and reserve. The croutons can be made a day ahead of time and stored in an airtight container at room temperature.
4. In a large mixing bowl, combine the cooked croutons, diced tomatoes, basil, and parsley. Add 3 tablespoons of the vinaigrette, and toss, slowly adding more vinaigrette until the bread is just moistened. Serve immediately.

✶ *Makes 4 to 6 servings*

Balsamic Vinaigrette

From the kitchen of Giovanna Roy

For this basic vinaigrette, I use the same recipe that my Nana used, but sometimes I alter the fresh herbs according to my taste and what is available. I often substitute fresh chives for the basil.

1 clove garlic, crushed
¼ teaspoon salt
2 tablespoons balsamic vinegar
½ teaspoon dry mustard or Dijon
½ to ¾ cup virgin olive oil
2 tablespoons chopped fresh parsley
2 tablespoons chopped fresh basil
Pepper

1. In a small bowl, combine the garlic, salt, vinegar, and mustard. Gradually whisk in the olive oil. If using a jar, place the garlic, salt, vinegar, mustard, and oil in the jar, replace the lid, and shake the jar vigorously.
2. Stir in the parsley, basil, and pepper to taste. Taste and adjust the seasonings.

✶ *Makes ¾ cup*

Copper Penny Salad

From the kitchen of C.W.

The sliced carrot rounds give this salad its name.

2 pounds carrots, peeled
1 large green pepper, chopped
1 large onion, sliced into thin rings
1 (10¾-ounce) can tomato soup
½ cup salad oil
1 cup sugar
¾ cup vinegar
1 teaspoon dry mustard
1 tablespoon Worcestershire sauce
1 teaspoon salt
½ teaspoon pepper

1. Bring 3 quarts of water to a boil in a large pot over high heat. Add the whole carrots, and cook until just tender. Remove from the heat, and transfer to a colander. Rinse with cold water to stop the cooking process and drain. Set aside, and allow to cool. When cooled, slice the carrots in ¼-inch- to ½-inch-thick slices.
2. Combine the carrot slices, green pepper, and onion rings in a medium bowl.
3. In a small bowl, whisk together the tomato soup, oil, sugar, vinegar, dry mustard, Worcestershire sauce, salt, and pepper. Mix well, and add to the bowl with the vegetables. Cover and refrigerate for 24 hours. Serve chilled.

✶ *Makes 10 to 15 servings*

Fresh Corn Salad

From the kitchen of C.M.

This tried and true recipe is a great showcase for fresh tomatoes, corn, and peppers. It is even better when those veggies come from your own garden.

8 ears sweet corn, cooked
½ cup olive oil
¼ cup cider vinegar
1 tablespoon lemon juice
1 teaspoon sugar
¼ cup minced fresh parsley
2 teaspoons dried basil or 3 tablespoons chopped fresh basil
2 large tomatoes, peeled and chopped
½ cup chopped green pepper
½ cup chopped celery
½ cup minced green onions
Salad greens

1. With a sharp knife, cut the corn kernels from the cobs. In a medium bowl, mix the oil, vinegar, lemon juice, sugar, parsley, and basil. Add the corn, tomatoes, pepper, celery, green onions, and toss. Cover and refrigerate several hours.
2. To serve, line a salad bowl with the greens, and fill with the corn salad.

∗ *Makes 8 to 10 servings*

Green Jell-O Salad

From the kitchen of B.M.

My husband and I are both from Utah; we were raised on Green Jell-O Salad, and we both love it. Everyone has her own way of making it. I've had it with apples, celery, marshmallows, Cheddar cheese, peaches, pears, even green pepper. No two Utahans will make theirs exactly the same—unless, of course, it's a family recipe. This version has been in my family for several generations.

1 cup boiling water
1 (4-ounce) package lime-flavored Jell-O
½ cup cold water
⅛ teaspoon salt
1 (8¼-ounce) can crushed pineapple in syrup, not drained
1 cup shredded carrot

1. In a medium bowl, combine the boiling water and Jell-O. Stir until the Jell-O is dissolved. Stir in the cold water, salt, and pineapple. Refrigerate 40 minutes.
2. Stir in the shredded carrot, and transfer the mixture to a casserole dish for serving. Refrigerate about 3 hours.

∗ *Makes 6 to 8 servings*

Rhubarb Salad

From the kitchen of Marilyn Woods

My mom used to make this when rhubarb was in season.

3 cups chopped fresh rhubarb
½ cup sugar
¼ teaspoon salt
2 (4-ounce) packages strawberry Jell-O
2 cups cold water
2 cups finely chopped celery
¼ cup lemon juice

1. In a heavy saucepan over low heat, combine the rhubarb, sugar, and salt. Cook without adding water and without stirring until the rhubarb is tender, about 15 minutes. Increase the heat, bring the mixture to a rapid boil, and remove from the heat.
2. Add the Jell-O, and stir gently. Stir in the water, celery, and lemon juice. Refrigerate for 3 to 4 hours to set.

✶ *Makes 8 servings*

Old-fashioned Applesauce

From the kitchen of L.L.

I probably make this old-fashioned, chunky applesauce once a week during the winter. It's one of my favorite recipes. If you are tempted to skip the mace, don't; it really makes this applesauce taste great—as does using real apple cider instead of apple juice.

1 to 1½ cups sugar
1 tablespoon ground cinnamon
1 teaspoon ground nutmeg
1 teaspoon mace
Pinch of salt
10 to 15 apples (such as Granny Smith or Golden Delicious), peeled and sliced
1 cup apple cider, apple juice, or water
2 teaspoons unsalted butter

1. In a small bowl, whisk together the sugar, cinnamon, nutmeg, mace, and salt. In a slow cooker, layer the apples with the sugar/spice mixture, apple cider, and butter. Cook on high heat for 2 hours, stirring every half hour until the apples are soft and break up.
2. Cool, place in glass or plastic containers, and refrigerate.

Serving ideas: While delicious cold, the applesauce may also be served warm in a bowl with a scoop of ice cream on top.

✶ *Makes 2 quarts*

Grandma Shoemaker's Cranberry Relish

From the kitchen of Maribeth Pittman

Be sure to make this relish one day ahead. Use a hand-turned food grinder, if possible. Although you can do this in a food processor, the texture is better with the old-fashioned model. I often vary the amount of sugar I use according to the sweetness of the fruit and my own taste, which runs to the sweet side.

1 pound fresh cranberries, washed, picked over, and patted dry
2 navel oranges, washed, and cut into sixths
2 firm, crisp, unpeeled apples, cored, and cut into sixths
1½ to 2 cups sugar
1 cup chopped pecans (optional)

1. In a food processor or food grinder, process or grind the cranberries, and transfer them to a large bowl. Grind or process the oranges, with their peel, and transfer them to the bowl with the cranberries. Grind or process the apple pieces, with the skins on, and transfer them to the bowl.
2. Stir to combine the ground fruit. Mix in the sugar, a little at a time, and taste to adjust sweetness. Stir in the nuts, cover, and chill for 24 hours before serving.

* *Makes about 1 quart*

Grandma Rosella's Haroset

From the kitchen of Stacia Jesner

Haroset is one of the key items for the seder plate at Passover. It represents the bricks and mortar that the Hebrew slaves used to build the Pharaoh's monuments during their captivity in Egypt. In keeping with my husband's family's tradition, we also serve a big bowl of it with matzo as an hors d'oeurve before we begin our seder. Since the readings can take almost an hour before the main meal begins, it helps to tide everyone over.

¼ to ½ pound walnuts
2 small apples, peeled and cored
½ cup kosher red wine
3 tablespoons honey

1. Blend the walnuts, apples, wine, and honey in a blender or food processor until the mixture is coarsely ground and sticks together. This keeps for a week in the refrigerator.

⁎ *Makes 8 servings*

Cranberry Horseradish Relish

From the kitchen of Giovanna Roy

This relish has real zip. I make this every year because my hubby loves horseradish. I always think he's going to be the only one eating it, but to my surprise, everyone always loves this, even the kids.

2 cups cranberries
½ cup sugar
¼ cup prepared horseradish
1 tablespoon lemon juice

1. In the bowl of a food processor, place the cranberries and sugar, and process until finely chopped.
2. Transfer to a mixing bowl. Stir in the horseradish and lemon juice. Cover and chill for at least 24 hours. This can be made five days ahead.

✶ *Makes about ¾ quart*

6

Breads and Muffins

Mom's Famous White Bread

From the kitchen of C.T.

Here's Mom's Famous White Bread recipe. It's been in her recipe box forever.

1 (1¼-ounce) package active dry yeast
1 teaspoon plus 2 tablespoons sugar
1 plus ¼ cups warm water
1 cup milk, scalded
2 teaspoons salt
7 to 7½ cups all-purpose flour

1. Stir the yeast and 1 teaspoon sugar into the ¼ cup lukewarm water. Set aside to proof for 10 minutes.
2. In a large mixing bowl, place the scalded milk and the remaining 1 cup water. Gradually add the remaining 2 tablespoons sugar, salt, and half the flour. Mix well. Add the proofed yeast and the remaining flour, and mix well.
3. Turn the dough onto a lightly floured surface, and knead until smooth and elastic, about 10 minutes. Shape the dough into a ball, and place it in a well-greased bowl. Turn the dough over to coat with oil. Cover with a damp tea towel, and let the dough rise in a warm place until double in bulk, about 1 hour.
4. Divide the dough in half, shape each portion into a loaf, and place in loaf pans. Cover with a damp towel, and let rise in a warm place until double in bulk, about 45 minutes.
5. Preheat the oven to 375°.
6. Bake until evenly brown and the bread sounds hollow when rapped with a knuckle on top, about 40 to 45 minutes. Remove from the loaf pans, and transfer to a wire rack to cool.

* *Makes 2 loaves*

Portuguese Sweet Bread (Masa)

From the kitchen of Sherry Knackstept

This is my great-grandmother's recipe. During Easter, we pushed hard-boiled eggs into the loaves before baking. At other times, we added raisins to the dough. But most of the time, we enjoyed it just plain.

2 (¼-ounce) packages active dry yeast
¼ cup warm water
1 cup sugar
1 cup scalded milk
4 tablespoons butter
1 teaspoon salt
3 eggs, well beaten
5 plus 1½ cups all-purpose flour, sifted
1 tablespoon butter, melted

1. Dissolve the yeast in the warm water. In a very large bowl, mix together the sugar, hot milk, the 4 tablespoons butter, and salt. Stir until the butter is melted. When the mixture is cooled to lukewarm, beat in the eggs and yeast mixture.
2. Add 5 cups of the flour, 1 cup at a time, into the liquid mixture, beating until smooth. Remove from the bowl, and place the dough on a flat, lightly floured surface. Knead the remaining 1½ cups flour into the dough, a little at a time, until the dough is smooth and little air bubbles form on the surface, about 10 minutes. Shape the dough into a ball.
3. Place the melted butter in a very large, clean bowl. Transfer the dough to the bowl, and round up the dough to coat the whole surface with melted butter. Cover with a damp tea towel, and set aside to rise in a warm place until the dough doubles in size. This will take about 1 hour.
4. Preheat the oven to 350°.
5. Remove the dough from the bowl, and cut into rolls or loaves. Place on a greased baking sheet or in two greased 9 x 5-inch loaf pans. Bake until brown and the loaves sound hollow when tapped, about 30 minutes.

∗ *Makes 24 rolls or 2 loaves*

Granny Lewis's Banana Bread

From the kitchen of C.B.

My grandmother's recipe is a real old-fashioned way to make banana bread—so simple and so good. When I would make this with my kids, they always thought the vinegar was the magic ingredient because it made the soda foam. To some extent they were right, because it's the ingredient that distinguishes this as an "old" recipe, harkening back to times when, rather than purchase buttermilk, cooks soured their own milk.

1 cup sugar
2 eggs
½ cup butter
3 ripe bananas, mashed
2 cups all-purpose flour
½ cup nuts (optional)
1 teaspoon baking soda
1 tablespoon vinegar
1 tablespoon milk or cream

1. Preheat the oven to 350°. Grease and flour a 9 x 5-inch loaf pan.
2. In a large bowl of an electric mixer, beat the sugar, eggs, and butter until light and fluffy. Slowly add the bananas, and mix well. Stir in the flour and nuts, if using.
3. In a separate bowl, place the baking soda, and then add the vinegar and milk (in *that* order), and mix to combine. Add this liquid mixture to the batter, and mix well.
4. Pour into the prepared pan. Bake until a toothpick inserted in the middle comes out clean, about 1 hour. Remove from the oven, and let rest in the pan for 10 minutes. Remove from the pan, and transfer to a wire rack to cool.

✶ *Makes 1 loaf*

Zucchini Nut Bread

From the kitchen of C.J.

This bread gets better as it ages. It can be stored in the refrigerator for two weeks or longer. It is simply to die for.

2 cups shredded, unpeeled zucchini
3 eggs
1 cup vegetable oil
1 cup sugar
⅓ cup molasses
2 teaspoons vanilla extract
2¼ cups all-purpose flour or 2 cups all-purpose flour and ¼ cup whole wheat flour
1 teaspoon salt
1 teaspoon baking soda
½ teaspoon baking powder
2 teaspoons ground cinnamon
1 cup raisins
1 cup chopped nuts

1. Preheat the oven to 350°. Grease and flour two 9 x 5-inch loaf pans.
2. With a coarse grater, shred the zucchini. If the zucchini is extremely watery, place it in a colander or sieve to drain while preparing the batter.
3. In a large bowl of an electric mixer, beat the eggs until frothy. Slowly add the oil, sugar, molasses, and vanilla, and beat until thick and foamy.
4. In a separate small bowl, combine the flour, salt, baking soda, baking powder, and cinnamon. Mix well, and add to the egg mixture. Stir until blended. Add the zucchini, raisins, and nuts. Mix gently.
5. Divide the batter between the two prepared pans. Bake until a toothpick inserted comes out clean, about 1 hour. Remove from the oven, and let rest in the pans for 10 minutes. Carefully remove from the pans, and transfer to a wire rack to cool. Chill before slicing.

✶ *Makes 2 loaves*

Spicy Pineapple-Zucchini Bread

From the kitchen of Marilyn Woods

I have tried many bread recipes, but this one is my favorite. It calls for powdered sugar frosting, but I don't think it needs it. It can be frozen in a zipper-top plastic bag or wrapped in plastic wrap.

3 eggs
2 cups sugar
1 cup vegetable oil
2 teaspoons vanilla extract
2 cups coarsely shredded, unpeeled zucchini
1 (8-ounce) can crushed pineapple, well drained
3 cups all-purpose flour
½ teaspoon salt
2 teaspoons baking soda
½ teaspoon baking powder
2 teaspoons ground cinnamon
1 teaspoon ground nutmeg
½ teaspoon allspice
1 cup chopped walnuts

1. Preheat the oven to 350°. Grease and flour two 9 x 5-inch loaf pans.
2. Beat the eggs lightly in a large bowl of an electric mixer. Slowly add the sugar, oil, and vanilla. Beat until thick and foamy. Remove the bowl from the mixer. By hand, stir in the zucchini and pineapple.
3. In a separate bowl, combine the flour, salt, baking soda, baking powder, cinnamon, nutmeg, allspice, and nuts. Using a wooden spoon, mix well, and stir into the zucchini mixture until well blended.
4. Divide the mixture between two prepared pans. Bake in the oven until a toothpick inserted in the center comes out clean, about 1 hour. Remove from the oven, and let cool in the pans for 10 minutes. Remove from the pans, and transfer to a wire rack to cool.

✶ *Makes 2 loaves*

Mom's Cloud Biscuits

From the kitchen of M.P.

My mom always used an old metal baking powder can to cut out these biscuits. I have it now and use it sometimes. You can use a biscuit cutter or the rim of a glass.

2 cups all-purpose flour
4 teaspoons baking powder
1 teaspoon sugar
½ teaspoon salt
½ cup cold butter
1 large egg, beaten
⅔ cup whole milk

1. Preheat the oven to 400°.
2. In the bowl of a food processor, place the flour, baking powder, sugar, and salt. Pulse twice to mix. Add the butter cut into pieces. Process until the mixture becomes a coarse meal, about 5 to 8 pulses. Transfer to a large mixing bowl.
3. In a separate small bowl, combine the beaten egg and milk. Using a fork, stir the liquid into the flour mixture.
4. Turn the dough onto a flat, lightly floured surface, and knead lightly. With a floured rolling pin, roll out to ½-inch thickness. Cut out rounds with a 2- to 3-inch biscuit cutter. Gather the scraps together, and pat into another biscuit shape.
5. Place the biscuits on a baking sheet with the edges touching. Bake for 10 to 15 minutes.

✶ *Makes 12 biscuits*

Cinnamon Rolls

From the kitchen of Giovanna Roy

This recipe is a little different, but very good. The addition of mashed potatoes makes a nice, soft dough.

1½ cups warm water
½ cup granulated sugar
½ cup vegetable oil
½ cup mashed potatoes, unseasoned and without milk
1 egg
2 teaspoons salt
3 (¼-ounce) packages active dry yeast
3 tablespoons nonfat dry milk powder
5½ to 6 cups all-purpose flour
¾ cup firmly packed brown sugar
1½ tablespoons ground cinnamon
⅓ cup butter, softened

1. Grease three 8-inch or 9-inch round baking pans.
2. Combine the warm water, granulated sugar, oil, potatoes, egg, salt, and yeast in a large bowl of an electric mixer. Mix well. Add the milk powder and 3 cups of the flour. Beat for 3 minutes. Gradually add the remaining 2½ to 3 cups flour, and when the dough is workable, transfer to a lightly floured surface.
3. Knead until smooth and elastic, about 10 minutes. Shape the dough into a large ball, transfer it to a well-greased bowl, and turn it over in the bowl to coat with the oil. Cover with a damp tea towel, and let rise in a warm place until doubled in bulk, about 1½ hours.
4. Punch the dough down, and turn the ball of dough over in the bowl. Cover and let rise again until doubled in bulk, about 1 hour.
5. In a small bowl, mix the brown sugar and cinnamon.
6. Punch down the dough again, and transfer it to a lightly floured surface. Divide into thirds. Roll each third into an 8 x 12-inch rectangle. Evenly spread the butter on each portion, and sprinkle with the cinnamon-sugar mixture. Starting at the short side, tightly roll up the dough in jelly roll fashion. Cut off slices 1 inch thick, and arrange them flat on the prepared pans. Cover and let rise for an hour.
7. Preheat the oven to 400°.
8. Bake the rolls for 15 minutes, then reduce the heat to 350°, and continue baking until evenly brown, about 10 to 15 minutes longer. Remove from the oven, and invert the pans onto wax-paper-lined wire racks. Let the rolls cool completely.

✶ *Makes about 27 rolls*

Southern Biscuits

From the kitchen of T.C.

My neighbor Linda makes these biscuits, and they're so good that I gave the recipe to my sister and mother. Beware! These Southern-style biscuits are in no way non-fattening or low calorie, and they may become a staple on your family's table as well.

2 cups self-rising flour
¼ cup plus 2 tablespoons lard or butter-flavored solid vegetable shortening
¾ cup buttermilk
1 large egg, beaten

1. Preheat the oven to 400°.
2. In the bowl of a food processor, place the flour and shortening cut into small pieces. Process until the mixture becomes a coarse meal, about 5 to 8 pulses. Transfer to a large mixing bowl.
3. In a small bowl, blend the buttermilk and egg. Using a fork, stir the buttermilk mixture into the flour mixture. Do *not* overmix.
4. Transfer the dough onto a flat, well-floured board. Lightly pat dough into a round about 1 inch thick. Cut into rounds with a 2- to 3-inch biscuit cutter. Gather the scraps together, and pat into another biscuit shape.
5. For soft biscuits, place in a greased 8-inch round cake pan with biscuit sides touching. For firm, crisp edges, place one inch apart on a baking sheet.
6. Bake until brown, about 10 to 12 minutes.

✶ *Makes 12 to 15 biscuits*

Pumpkin Nutmeg Rolls

From the kitchen of Carol Montague

Rather than popping the same old brown-n-serve rolls into the oven, why not make some wonderful yeast rolls? You are bound to get rave reviews. During the holiday season at my house, I make a variety of rolls, but this recipe always receives a lot of attention.

1 (¼-ounce) package active dry yeast
1 teaspoon plus ⅓ cup sugar
¾ cup lukewarm milk
7 to 8 cups all-purpose flour
½ teaspoon freshly grated nutmeg
1 teaspoon salt
¾ cup cold, unsalted butter, cut into small pieces
1 egg, beaten lightly
1 (16-ounce) can pumpkin purée
1 egg yolk beaten with 1 tablespoon water

1. Grease a 10-inch springform pan. In a small bowl, stir the yeast and 1 teaspoon sugar into the warm milk. Set aside until the mixture foams, about 5 to 10 minutes.
2. In a large bowl, combine 7 cups flour, nutmeg, salt, and the remaining ⅓ cup sugar. Mix well. Cut the butter into the flour until it resembles coarse meal. Add the beaten egg, pumpkin purée, and yeast mixture. Stir until well mixed.
3. Turn the dough onto a lightly floured surface, and knead, incorporating as much of the remaining 1 cup flour as necessary to prevent the dough from sticking. Knead until the dough is smooth and elastic, about 10 minutes. Shape the dough into a ball, and transfer it to a well-greased large bowl. Turn the dough over in the bowl to coat with oil. Cover with plastic wrap, and let rise in a warm place (about 80°) until doubled in bulk, about 1 to 1½ hours.
4. Transfer the dough to a lightly floured surface, and divide it into 14 equal portions. Shape each piece into a ball. Fit the balls into the prepared pan, cover with a damp tea towel, and let rise in a warm place until doubled in bulk, about 45 minutes.
5. Preheat the oven to 350°.
6. Brush the rolls with the egg yolk beaten with water, and bake on the center rack of the oven until golden brown, about 40 to 50 minutes. The bread is done when evenly brown on all sides and it sounds hollow when rapped with a knuckle on top. Remove the bread from the oven, and let the rolls cool slightly in pan, about 2 minutes. Remove outside of the pan, and let cool completely. Tastes best when slightly warm.

Note: The rolls may be made one week in advance and wrapped in foil and frozen. To reheat the rolls, bake at 350° until they are heated through, about 25 minutes.

✶ *Makes 14 rolls*

Myrtle's Butter Rolls

From the kitchen of D.N.

My mama made these rolls when I was a child, and the recipe was taught to her by her mother. The recipe is probably about 70 years old.

My mother and my 86-year-old aunt remember using freshly churned butter. I grew up on that kind, and it's a far cry from what you get in the stores these days. But even with store-bought butter, these are still delicious sweet rolls that I've loved for decades.

For the rolls:

2 cups all-purpose flour
3 teaspoons baking powder
1 teaspoon salt
1/3 cup solid vegetable shortening
2/3 cup buttermilk
6 tablespoons butter, softened
6 tablespoons sugar

For the sauce:

4 cups milk
1 cup sugar
1½ teaspoons vanilla extract
2 tablespoons butter

1. Preheat the oven to 400°.
2. In a large bowl of an electric mixer, blend together the flour, baking powder, salt, shortening, and buttermilk. Place the dough on a lightly floured surface, and knead with your hands until fully blended and the dough is a little firmer than biscuit dough.
3. Using a rolling pin, roll out the dough into a 9 x 13-inch rectangle.
4. With a knife or rubber scraper, carefully spread the softened butter over the entire surface of the dough. Sprinkle with the sugar.
5. Starting with the 13-inch side, roll up lengthwise, jelly roll style. Place cut side down on a 9 x 13-inch baking pan.
6. For the sauce, combine the milk, sugar, vanilla, and butter in a large saucepan over medium-low heat. Cook until hot and the butter is melted. Be careful not to boil. Pour over the jelly roll.
7. Bake until lightly browned on top and the milk mixture has thickened slightly to form a sauce, about 30 minutes.
8. Cut into servings immediately, and spoon the sauce over each roll.

Variation: Although we never did, some people sprinkle 1 teaspoon cinnamon over the dough and softened butter before they roll the dough.

✶ *Makes 8 rolls*

Mom's Blueberry Muffins

From the kitchen of Giovanna Roy

My mom (now 80 years old) got this recipe from a neighbor when she was young. The way my mom tells it, she had to beg this lady for about a year to get it because it was her "special" recipe. Of course, being my mom, she couldn't help but tinker with the recipe to make it even better.

4 cups flour
4 teaspoons baking powder
½ teaspoon salt
1 teaspoon nutmeg
1 cup unsalted butter
2 cups sugar
4 eggs
2 teaspoons vanilla extract
2 tablespoons lemon juice
1⅓ cups milk
3 to 4 cups blueberries
Sugar to sprinkle on top

1. Preheat the oven to 350°. Line two 18-cup muffin tins with paper liners.
2. In a large bowl, sift together the flour, baking powder, salt, and nutmeg.
3. Cream the butter and sugar until light and fluffy in a large bowl of an electric mixer. Add the eggs one at a time, blending for a few seconds before adding the next one. Add the vanilla and lemon juice, and mix until blended. Add half the flour mixture, the milk, and then the second half of the flour mixture, mixing after each addition. Remove the bowl from the mixer, and add the blueberries, stirring in by hand.
4. Fill each cup of the muffin tins three-fourths of the way full with batter. Sprinkle with the sugar as desired. Bake for 15 to 18 minutes or until the muffins are light brown but not too golden.

✶ *Makes 36 muffins*

7

Cookies, Bars, and Candies

My Mom's Pecan Crescents (Butter Balls)

From the kitchen of Trina Cieply

Holidays would not be the same without these cookies. They are so light and airy that they melt in your mouth. They are everyone's favorite. Three dozen balls are never enough.

1 cup butter
4 tablespoons confectioners' sugar
1 teaspoon vanilla extract
2 cups sifted all-purpose flour
1 cup pecans, chopped
Confectioners' sugar for rolling

1. Preheat the oven to 350°.
2. In the large bowl of an electric mixer, beat together the butter and sugar until light and fluffy. Add vanilla. Add the flour, and mix well. By hand, fold in the nuts.
3. Shape the dough into small balls or crescents, and place them on ungreased cookie sheets. Bake until they begin to color, about 15 to 18 minutes. Remove from the oven, and roll in confectioners' sugar while still hot.

** Makes about 36 balls or 24 crescents*

Orange Delights

From the kitchen of Robin Nagel

My great-grandmother kept her cookie jar filled with these cookies. The recipe was handed down to her from her mother. My great-grandmother told us her mother had gotten it from someone before they moved over here from Germany. They moved here when my great-grandmother was eight years old. The only things they were able to bring over with them on the boat were very special things that would fit in a big trunk that my mother now has. I guess this recipe was one of those special things.

For the cookies:

3/4 cup butter
1 1/2 cups firmly packed brown sugar
2 eggs
1/2 cup buttermilk
1/2 teaspoon baking soda
3 cups all-purpose flour
1 1/2 teaspoons baking powder
1/4 teaspoon salt
1 teaspoon vanilla extract
1 1/2 teaspoons grated orange zest

For the icing:

1 1/2 teaspoons grated orange zest
1/3 cup orange juice
1 cup granulated sugar

1. Preheat the oven to 350°.
2. To make the cookies, beat together the butter and brown sugar in a large bowl of an electric mixer until light and fluffy. Add the eggs, and mix well.
3. In a small bowl, mix the buttermilk with baking soda until dissolved. Add to the batter, and mix well.
4. In a separate medium bowl, sift together the flour, baking powder, and salt. Gradually add to the batter. Add the vanilla and orange zest, and mix well.
5. Drop by teaspoonfuls onto a greased cookie sheet. Bake until set and lightly browned on edges, about 12 to 15 minutes.
6. To make the icing, in a small bowl, combine the orange zest, orange juice, and granulated sugar. Mix into a thin paste.
7. Remove the cookies from the oven, and while still hot, spread them with a thin layer of icing. Let cool to set.

✶ *Makes 36 cookies*

Pecan Tassies

From the kitchen of A.M.

For the pastry:

3 ounces cream cheese
½ cup butter
1¼ cups sifted all-purpose flour

For the filling:

1 egg
¾ cup firmly packed brown sugar
¼ teaspoon salt
1 tablespoon melted butter
½ teaspoon vanilla extract
1 cup pecans, chopped

1. Preheat the oven to 350°. Lightly grease miniature muffin tins for 2 dozen.
2. Beat together the cream cheese and butter in a large bowl of an electric mixer until light and fluffy. Add the flour, and mix well. If necessary, add ½ teaspoon ice water to bind the dough. The dough should resemble pie crust.
3. Divide the dough into 24 balls, and mold into the muffin tins to form pie-like shells or pastry cups.
4. In a separate mixing bowl, combine the egg, brown sugar, salt, melted butter, and vanilla. Mix well.
5. Pour the mixture into the pastry cups, filling them three-fourths full. Top each cup with a rounded teaspoon of pecans. Bake for 20 minutes.

✶ *Makes 24 cups*

My Mom's Whoopie Pies

From the kitchen of Giovanna Roy

Growing up in Lancaster County, I had the privilege of sampling some wonderful Pennsylvania Dutch cooking. My grandmother and my mother were excellent cooks, and I am thankful for the rich heritage and wonderful recipes they gave me. I always enjoyed going to my grandmother's house, especially when she had whoopie pies in the freezer. She would make extra and freeze them. Every year, my mom would bake a birthday treat for me to take to school and share with my classmates, and every year I asked for whoopie pies. What fun I had helping to make the chocolate cakes and spreading the cream filling between them.

Whoopie pies also hold another special memory for me. A little less than three weeks before my oldest son's due date, I made a big batch of these soft cookie sandwiches, putting as many as I could in the freezer to enjoy later. I had no sooner finished cleaning up and eating a whoopie pie when my son decided he wanted to join our family. He was born several hours later. So what are whoopie pies like? They are similar to Little Debbie Cakes, but so much better. Try this recipe and you will see for yourself.

For the cookies:

2 cups granulated sugar
1 cup butter
2 whole eggs plus 2 egg yolks
2 teaspoons vanilla extract
4 cups all-purpose flour
1 cup unsweetened cocoa powder
2 teaspoons baking soda
½ teaspoon salt
1 cup buttermilk

For the filling:

2 egg whites
1 cup butter, softened
1 teaspoon vanilla extract
4 tablespoons milk
1 box confectioners' sugar

1. Preheat the oven to 350°. Grease two cookie sheets.
2. To make the cookies, in a large bowl of an electric mixer, beat together the sugar and butter until light and fluffy. Add the two whole eggs and two eggs yolks (reserving the whites for the filling), and beat well after each addition. Stir in the vanilla.
3. In a separate bowl, sift together the flour, cocoa powder, baking soda, and salt.
4. Alternately add the flour mixture and buttermilk to the batter, beating well after each addition. The batter will be stiff. (If it is too thin, add a little more flour, ¼ cup at a time.)

5. Drop by tablespoonfuls onto the cookie sheets. Bake until a toothpick inserted in the cookies comes out clean, about 8 to 10 minutes. Transfer to a wire rack to cool completely.
6. To make the filling, beat the egg whites until stiff in the clean bowl of an electric mixer. Beat in the butter and vanilla. Add the milk and then the confectioners' sugar. Beat until smooth.
7. To assemble, spread some filling on the bottom side of one cookie, and top with another cookie as if it were a sandwich. Repeat with the remaining cookies and filling. Store in the refrigerator or freezer.

★ *Makes about 60 sandwiches*

Granny's Pumpkin Cookies

From the kitchen of P.N.

My grandmother's recipe for these cookies was simply a list of ingredients. But with a little help from a friend, I have reconstructed the instructions. I don't recall ever making these with my grandmother—but I have extremely fond memories of eating them.

1½ cups sugar
½ cup butter
1 egg
1 cup canned pumpkin
1 teaspoon vanilla extract
2½ cups all-purpose flour
1 teaspoon ground nutmeg
1 teaspoon ground cinnamon
1 teaspoon baking powder
1 teaspoon baking soda
½ teaspoon salt
1 cup chocolate chips
1 cup pecans, coarsely chopped

1. Preheat the oven to 375°. Grease several cookie sheets.
2. In a large bowl of an electric mixer, beat together the sugar and butter until light and fluffy. Beat in the egg, pumpkin, and vanilla.
3. In a separate bowl, whisk together the flour, nutmeg, cinnamon, baking powder, baking soda, and salt. Gradually add the flour mixture to the batter. Mix well. Stir in the chocolate chips and pecans.
4. Drop by tablespoonfuls onto the prepared cookie sheets. Bake until golden brown, about 8 to 10 minutes. Transfer to a wire rack to cool.

∗ *Makes 24 to 36 cookies*

Holiday Cut-outs

From the kitchen of Ellen Rofkar

I have to make this old family recipe every year. If I don't, I am sure to get yelled at. These classic holiday cookies bring joy to the whole family because they are as fun to decorate as they are to eat. To decorate with cinnamon candies or other similar decorations, sprinkle on top of the cookies before baking. Otherwise, bake plain and paint with frosting and festive decorations after they are cooled.

3 cups all-purpose flour
1 teaspoon baking powder
½ teaspoon salt
1 cup butter, softened
¾ cup sugar
1 egg
2 tablespoons cream or milk
1½ teaspoons vanilla extract

1. Preheat the oven to 400°.
2. Sift together the flour, baking powder, and salt. In a large bowl of an electric mixer, beat together the butter and sugar until light and fluffy. Add the egg, milk, and vanilla, and beat well. Gradually blend in the flour mixture. Mix well. Cover the dough and chill for 1 hour.
3. Remove the dough from the refrigerator, and divide into thirds. Transfer to a lightly floured surface. Roll out each portion into a ¼-inch-thick rectangle, and cut out holiday shapes using assorted cookie cutters. Carefully transfer to ungreased cookie sheets.
4. Bake until set but not brown, about 5 to 8 minutes. Watch carefully to prevent burning. Remove from the oven, and transfer to a wire rack to cool. When completely cool, paint with frosting, and decorate.

∗ *Makes 36 cookies*

Lemon Crinkles

From the kitchen of Caryn Dubelko

When a friend needed a lemon cookie for a reception following a first communion, these perfect cookies came to mind. They are crisp on the edges and chewy on the inside—a light and sweet delight.

¾ cup butter
1¼ cups sugar
1 egg
¼ cup evaporated milk
2 cups sifted all-purpose flour
1 teaspoon baking powder
1 teaspoon salt
¼ teaspoon baking soda
¼ teaspoon yellow food coloring
2 teaspoons lemon extract
Extra sugar for rolling

1. In a large bowl of an electric mixer, beat together the butter and sugar until light and fluffy. Beat in the egg and milk.
2. In a separate bowl, whisk together the flour, baking powder, salt, and baking soda. Gradually add the flour mixture to the batter, and mix well. Mix in the food coloring and lemon extract. Cover and refrigerate until the dough is firm, about 30 to 60 minutes.
3. Preheat the oven to 350°.
4. With wet hands, shape the dough into 1-inch balls. Roll in the sugar. Place two inches apart on an ungreased cookie sheet. Bake until crisp on the edges, about 12 to 13 minutes.

✶ *Makes 24 cookies*

My Mother-in-law's Molasses Cookies

From the kitchen of Robin Nagel

My mother-in-law used to make these molasses cookies. Unfortunately I never knew her, though I know I would have loved her. She passed away when my husband was just a teenager, but this is one of her many recipes that continue to live on.

4½ cups all-purpose flour
2 teaspoons baking soda
3 teaspoons ground ginger
1 teaspoon salt
1 teaspoon ground cinnamon
1 teaspoon ground cloves
1 cup butter, softened
1 cup firmly packed brown sugar
2 eggs, well beaten
¾ to 1 cup molasses
¾ cup buttermilk

1. Sift together the flour, baking soda, ginger, salt, cinnamon, and cloves.
2. In a large bowl of an electric mixer, beat together the butter and brown sugar until light and fluffy. Add the eggs, molasses, and buttermilk, and mix well. Gradually add the flour mixture, and beat until smooth. Cover and refrigerate for at least 1 hour. (The dough can be chilled for 6 to 8 hours.)
3. Preheat the oven to 400°.
4. Transfer the dough to a lightly floured surface, and roll out until about ¼ inch thick. Dip a 3-inch cookie cutter into flour, and cut the dough into cookies. Place two inches apart on an ungreased baking sheet, and bake until firm and lightly browned on the edges, about 12 minutes. Transfer to a wire rack to cool.

✶ *Makes 36 cookies*

"I Dare You to Eat Three of These" Chocolate Chip Cookies

From the kitchen of Susan Hahn

These cookies were a staple of my childhood. My mother would mix the ingredients together, and I would volunteer to roll the dough into balls to put on the cookie sheet. Of course, half the dough never made it to the oven. My kids are just the same—they love cookies, but they love the batter even more. If you're worried about allowing your kids to eat raw eggs, use one of the egg substitutes instead. What's childhood without cookie dough?

1 cup granulated sugar
1 cup firmly packed brown sugar
¾ cup shortening
2 eggs
1 teaspoon vanilla extract
2 cups flour
2 cups quick-cooking oats
1 teaspoon baking powder
1 teaspoon salt
1 package semisweet chocolate chips
1 cup finely chopped walnuts (optional)

1. Preheat the oven to 350°.
2. Cream the granulated sugar, brown sugar, shortening, eggs, and vanilla together. Then mix in the flour, oats, baking powder, and salt. Add the chocolate chips (and nuts, if you like them).
3. Roll the dough into balls. Place on an ungreased cookie sheet. Bake for 12 to 14 minutes.

✶ *Makes 2 dozen cookies*

Oatmeal Lace Cookies

From the kitchen of Susan Hahn

My grandmother made these thin, lacy cookies. She used to say they were like snowflakes because each one was different. They look really pretty on a plate, and they are lovely to serve with tea.

1½ cups firmly packed brown sugar
1 egg, beaten
½ cup melted butter
1 teaspoon vanilla extract
½ teaspoon salt
1 cup quick-cooking oatmeal
½ cup currants soaked in brandy (optional)
1 teaspoon freshly ground cinnamon (optional)
1 teaspoon ground cardamom (optional)

1. Preheat the oven to 325°.
2. Cream together the sugar, egg, melted butter, vanilla, and salt. Mix in the oatmeal, stirring the batter well. Add the currants, cinnamon, and cardamom if desired.
3. Drop spoonfuls of the batter onto an ungreased cookie sheet, leaving room for the cookies to spread out. Bake until the cookies are light golden brown, about 12 minutes. Remove the cookies from the sheet, and transfer to a wire rack to cool.

✶ *Makes 4 dozen cookies*

Pam's Frosted Chocolate Nut Drop Cookies

From the kitchen of Giovanna Roy

My dearest friend gave me this recipe years ago, and it's one of my favorite cookies. It is to me what a holiday cookie should be: sweet, a little special, and super delicious. I simply cannot resist these cookies when they are around. Needless to say, I make them only at Christmas—if I made them more frequently, I'd go up two sizes in my jeans.

For the cookies:

2½ cups all-purpose flour
½ teaspoon baking powder
1 teaspoon salt
1 cup milk
3 tablespoons white vinegar
2 cups packed brown sugar
1 cup butter, softened
2 eggs, beaten
2 teaspoons vanilla extract
4 squares unsweetened chocolate, melted
2 cups chopped walnuts

For the frosting:

1 pound confectioners' sugar
½ cup butter, softened
1 teaspoon vanilla extract
3 tablespoons warm milk
2 squares unsweetened chocolate, melted

1. Preheat the oven to 350°. Grease a baking sheet.
2. To make the cookies, sift together the flour, baking powder, and salt.
3. In a small bowl, mix the milk with the vinegar to sour.
4. In a large bowl of an electric mixer, beat together the sugar and butter until light and fluffy. Add the eggs and vanilla, and beat to combine. Alternately add the flour mixture and soured milk to the batter. Add the chocolate and nuts. Mix well.
5. Drop by teaspoonfuls onto the baking sheet, and bake for 12 to 15 minutes.
6. Remove from the oven, and let rest on the baking sheet until the cookies are set, about 3 minutes. With a spatula, transfer the cookies to a wire rack to cool.
7. To make the frosting, in a medium bowl, beat together the confectioners' sugar, butter, vanilla, and milk until light and fluffy and of spreading consistency. When the cookies are cool, ice with the frosting. Decorate with a fork dipped into the melted chocolate to drizzle the chocolate in squiggles or lines on top of each cookie.

✶ *Makes 36 cookies*

Grandma's Sugar-Raisin Cookies

From the kitchen of J.M.

1½ cups raisins
1½ cups sugar
1 cup butter
2 eggs
1 teaspoon vanilla extract
3 cups all-purpose flour
1 teaspoon baking powder
1 teaspoon baking soda
½ teaspoon salt
½ teaspoon nutmeg
½ cup sugar for rolling

1. Preheat the oven to 400°. Grease two cookie sheets.
2. In a saucepan over medium heat, place the raisins with barely enough water to cover. Simmer until the water is absorbed, and remove from heat. Set aside to cool. (The raisins can be prepared one day ahead and refrigerated until needed.)
3. In a large bowl of an electric mixer, beat together the sugar and butter until light and fluffy. Add the eggs and vanilla, and beat thoroughly.
4. Sift together the flour, baking powder, baking soda, salt, and nutmeg. Add the flour mixture to the batter. Stir in the raisins, and mix well.
5. To form the cookies, roll 1 tablespoonful of dough into a ball. Roll in the sugar, and place two inches apart on the prepared cookie sheet. Flatten each cookie with a glass dipped in sugar. Bake until lightly brown, about 10 minutes.

∗ *Makes about 72 cookies*

Potato Chip Cookies

From the kitchen of Amy Steffan

A friend gave me this recipe, and I made some modifications. I can remember when she told me that she was making "potato chip" cookies—I gave her a look as if she were crazy. They actually taste much better than they sound. I always triple this recipe because it never seems to make enough of these cookies. I also like to use rippled chips, and sunflower kernels instead of nuts.

½ cup butter, room temperature
⅓ cup sugar
¾ teaspoon vanilla extract
1 cup all-purpose flour
⅓ cup crushed potato chips
⅓ cup chopped walnuts or pecans
Granulated sugar for dipping
Confectioners' sugar for sifting

1. Preheat the oven to 350°.
2. In a large bowl of an electric mixer, beat together the butter, sugar, and vanilla until light and fluffy. Slowly add the flour, and beat until blended. Stir in the potato chips and nuts.
3. Shape into 1-inch balls. Place three inches apart on an ungreased cookie sheet. Flatten the cookies with the bottom of a glass that is dipped in the granulated sugar.
4. Bake until the edges are lightly browned, about 12 to 15 minutes. With a spatula, transfer the cookies to a wire rack to cool. While slightly warm, sift the confectioners' sugar over the cookies.

✶ *Makes 24 to 30 cookies*

Ranger Cookies

From the kitchen of N.D.

Here's a recipe I used when I cooked at a summer camp years ago. They always came out nice and chewy. Just make sure you don't overbake them. You can also add raisins, dates, chocolate, or butterscotch chips if you want some variety.

1½ cups butter
1½ cups firmly packed brown sugar
1½ cups sugar
3 eggs
1½ teaspoons vanilla extract
3 cups all-purpose flour
1 tablespoon baking powder
1½ teaspoons baking soda
¾ teaspoon salt
3 cups rolled oats
1½ cups coconut
3 cups cornflakes

1. Preheat the oven to 350°.
2. In a large bowl of an electric mixer, beat together the butter, brown sugar, and sugar until light and fluffy. Add the eggs and vanilla.
3. Sift the flour, baking powder, baking soda, and salt together, and gradually add to the batter. Mix well. With a wooden spoon, stir in the oats and coconut and then the cornflakes.
4. Drop by tablespoonfuls onto an ungreased baking sheet about two inches apart. Bake until browned on edges, about 10 to 12 minutes.

✶ *Makes 54 cookies*

Applesauce Oatmeal Chocolate Chip Cookies

From the kitchen of N.D.

Mom always made a double or triple batch of these cake-type cookies when we were growing up because we ate them so fast (with a little help from our friends).

1 cup butter
½ cup granulated sugar
½ cup firmly packed brown sugar
2 eggs
1 cup unsweetened applesauce
1 teaspoon vanilla extract
2 cups all-purpose flour
1 teaspoon baking soda
1 teaspoon salt
2 teaspoons ground cinnamon
2 cups rolled oats
1 cup chocolate chips

1. Preheat the oven to 350°. Grease two baking sheets.
2. Beat together the butter, granulated sugar, and brown sugar in a large bowl of an electric mixer until light and fluffy. Stir in the eggs, applesauce, and vanilla.
3. In a separate bowl, whisk together the flour, baking soda, salt, and cinnamon. Stir the flour mixture into the batter. Mix well. Add the oatmeal and chocolate chips, and mix well.
4. Drop by teaspoonfuls onto the baking sheets. Bake until lightly browned, about 12 minutes. Transfer to a wire rack to cool.

✶ *Makes about 4 dozen cookies*

All-Night Drop Cookies

From the kitchen of Amanda Line

A terrific hot weather cookie. This recipe should be made late at night when the weather has cooled off. You preheat the oven, then turn it off, and leave the cookies in all night. When you get up, ta-da! Cookies without having to stand in a hot kitchen.

3 egg whites
1/8 teaspoon salt
1/3 cup sugar
1/2 cup mini chocolate chips

1. Preheat the oven to 350°. Line two baking sheets with foil, and grease the foil.
2. In a small bowl of an electric mixer, combine the egg whites with the salt at medium speed. Beat until soft peaks form. Gradually beat in the sugar, 1 tablespoon at a time, until stiff and glossy. Stir in the chocolate chips.
3. Drop by rounded tablespoonfuls onto foil-covered baking sheets. Place in the oven, shut the door, and turn off the heat. Do *not* open the door. Leave in the oven overnight. Remove from the oven, and store in airtight containers.

Variations: You can substitute chopped M&M's, mint chips, chopped nuts, or crushed peppermint candies for the chocolate chips.

✶ *Makes 30 cookies*

Anise Biscotti

From the kitchen of Giovanna Roy

Every time I eat one of these biscotti, I think of my Nana. My grandparents were a huge influence in my life; both were beautiful, loving, and gentle people. I remember sitting in their kitchen in the summer eating these biscotti. I can still picture that kitchen—the old refrigerator with the pull handle and the big oak table with fresh basil in the vase. My grandfather's beautiful roses stayed in his garden, but the basil always made it to the table. When we grandchildren came in from the garden with my grandfather, Nana's first question would be "Are you hungry?"

I have been making and eating these cookies for as long as I can remember. My Nana always had some on hand. Unlike the typical biscotti, which are baked twice, these are baked once as a log, sliced while still warm, and then drizzled with an anise glaze when cooled.

For the biscotti:

3¼ cups all-purpose flour
4 teaspoons baking powder
½ teaspoon salt
1 cup sugar
3 eggs
½ cup butter, melted
1 tablespoon pure anise extract

For the glaze:

2 to 3 cups confectioners' sugar, sifted
1 teaspoon pure anise extract
¼ to ⅓ cup milk or light cream

1. Preheat the oven to 350°. Line a cookie sheet with parchment paper.
2. To make the biscotti, in a large mixing bowl, whisk together the flour, baking powder, salt, and sugar.
3. In a small bowl, combine the eggs, butter, and anise, and mix well. Pour the egg/butter mixture into a well in the center of the flour mixture. Mix well with a wooden spoon or electric mixer until a thick dough forms.
4. Divide the dough in half, and shape into two long logs on the cookie sheet. Bake until the logs are lightly colored and a toothpick inserted in the center comes out clean, about 20 minutes.
5. Let cool slightly, and with a serrated-edge knife, cut at an angle ½-inch-thick slices. Try to keep the log together as much as possible.
6. To make the glaze, in a small bowl combine the confectioners' sugar, anise, and just enough milk to make a glaze that is slightly thick. Mix well, and with a spoon, drizzle the glaze over the logs. Let stand for 15 minutes to allow the glaze to set, and serve. Store in an air-tight container.

✶ *Makes 24 biscotti*

Banana Oat Squares

From the kitchen of Robyn Brown

This recipe whips up so easily and stays nice and soft for days, if you can make it last that long. It also makes a virtually fat-free breakfast treat.

2 medium-size ripe bananas, mashed
¼ cup skim milk
2 egg whites
1½ teaspoons vanilla or almond extract
1⅓ cups quick-cooking oats
¼ cup granulated sugar
¼ cup firmly packed brown sugar
2 teaspoons baking powder
1 teaspoon ground cinnamon
½ teaspoon baking soda
Cinnamon-sugar for dusting (optional)

1. Preheat the oven to 350°. Coat an 8-inch square baking pan with nonstick cooking spray.
2. In a large bowl of an electric mixer, combine the bananas, milk, egg whites, and vanilla.
3. In a separate medium bowl, combine the oats, granulated sugar, brown sugar, baking powder, cinnamon, and baking soda. Add the oat mixture to the banana mixture, and beat together until well blended.
4. Transfer to the prepared pan, and bake for 30 to 35 minutes. Remove from the oven, and let cool. Cut into squares, and sprinkle with cinnamon-sugar.

✶ *Makes 12 to 15 squares*

Chinese Chews

From the kitchen of Joan Russell

One of my mother's signature Christmas cookies is this chewy bar.

1 cup butter
2 cups sugar
4 eggs, beaten
2 teaspoons vanilla extract
2 cups all-purpose flour
1 teaspoon salt
About 1 pound whole Medjool dates (to yield 2 cups chopped dates)
1 cup chopped walnuts

1. Preheat the oven to 350°. Grease and flour a 9 x 13-inch pan.
2. In a large bowl of an electric mixer, beat together the butter and sugar until light and fluffy. Mix in the eggs and vanilla extract.
3. Combine the flour and salt in a separate bowl. Add the flour mixture to the batter, and blend until just combined.
4. Steam the dates for about 10 minutes to soften them. With a pair of scissors, cut the dates into bite-size pieces. Be sure to remove and discard the pits. Add the date pieces and walnuts to the batter, and mix well.
5. Pour the mixture into the prepared pan. Bake until the top is browned, about 45 to 50 minutes. Remove from the oven and let cool. When cool, cut into squares.

✶ *Makes 24 squares*

Congo Squares

From the kitchen of S. O.

My mom made these bar cookies often. She never included coconut, but I know plenty of folks who do.

Editor's note: The word "Congo" in the name of this recipe refers to Central Africa, which was once known as the Congo. That area of the world was once the primary source of cacao beans, the basic ingredient of chocolate.

⅔ cup butter
2¼ cups firmly packed brown sugar
3 eggs
2¾ cups all-purpose flour
2½ teaspoons baking powder
½ teaspoon salt
1 teaspoon vanilla extract
1 cup chopped pecans
1 (6-ounce) package chocolate chips
Confectioners' sugar for topping

1. Preheat the oven to 350°. Grease a 9 x 13-inch baking pan.
2. Beat together the butter and sugar in a large bowl of an electric mixer until light and fluffy. Add the eggs and beat well.
3. Sift the flour, baking powder, and salt together, and add to the batter. Beat well. Add the vanilla, nuts, and chocolate chips, and mix until fully combined.
4. Transfer to the prepared pan, and bake until lightly browned on the edges, about 40 minutes. Remove from the oven, and let cool. Sprinkle with the confectioners' sugar, and cut into bars.

✶ *Makes 24 bars*

Old-fashioned Brownies

From the kitchen of C.B.

My Granny Lewis was a great cook and taught me lots. Hers is the only brownie recipe I make. It is the old-fashioned type: chewy, not cake-like. I have included her original quantities, but I always add more cocoa since I love the big "rush" you get from the extra chocolate flavor.

I always double this recipe and bake in a 9 x 13-inch cake pan. Sometimes I dust the brownies with powdered sugar, and other times I top them with chocolate frosting (and I always use coffee as the liquid when I make the frosting).

1 cup sugar
4 to 6 tablespoons cocoa
½ cup butter
Pinch of salt
2 eggs
¾ cup all-purpose flour
1 cup nuts (optional)

1. Preheat the oven to 350°. Grease a 9 x 13-inch baking pan.
2. In a large bowl of an electric mixer, beat together the sugar, cocoa, butter, and salt until light and fluffy. Add the eggs and beat. Gradually stir in the flour and nuts. Mix well.
3. Spread the dough into the prepared pan. Bake until set and dull on top, about 25 minutes. Cut while warm. Let cool completely before frosting or dusting with sugar.

✶ *Makes 12 brownies*

Sand Art Brownie Mix

From the kitchen of Francine McCarthy

Here's a great gift idea—a brownie mix layered like sand art in a mason jar. Tie the top of the jar with raffia or ribbon, and affix the recipe. It's better than any store-bought mix and a lovely thing to have on hand in case you need a last-minute hostess gift.

1⅛ cups all-purpose flour
⅔ tablespoon salt
1 teaspoon baking powder
⅔ cup firmly packed brown sugar
⅔ cup granulated sugar
⅓ cup unsweetened cocoa powder
½ to ¾ cup walnuts
½ cup coconut
½ cup chocolate chips

1. In a 1-quart mason jar with a lid, layer the flour, then salt, and then baking powder. Top with layers of the brown sugar, granulated sugar, cocoa, walnuts, coconut, and chocolate chips—in that order.
2. Replace the lid, and decorate with ribbon and the following recipe:

Brownie Mix

Additional Ingredients:

3 eggs
1 teaspoon vanilla extract
¾ cup oil

Preheat the oven to 350°. Grease and flour a 9 x 9-inch pan.

Pour the contents of the jar into a large bowl. Stir to combine. Stir in the eggs, vanilla, and oil. Mix well. Pour into the prepared pan, and bake until a toothpick inserted in the center comes out clean, about 25 to 30 minutes.

✶ *Makes 12 brownies*

Dad's Peanut Brittle

From the kitchen of T.B.

Dad made this with us kids every year.

1 cup light corn syrup
2 cups sugar
½ cup water
2 cups raw Spanish peanuts
1½ tablespoons butter
1½ teaspoons vanilla extract
2 teaspoons baking soda

1. Grease a 17 x 15-inch jelly roll pan.
2. In a heavy pan over medium heat, combine the corn syrup, sugar, and water. Cook to the soft-ball stage (240° on a candy thermometer).
3. Add the peanuts, and stir well. Continue to cook until the hard-crack stage (301° on a candy thermometer). Remove from the heat, and stir in the butter, vanilla, and baking soda.
4. Pour into the prepared pan, and immediately turn over. With buttered hands, pull the mixture until very thin. Set aside, and let cool. When cooled, break into pieces.

✶ *Makes 24 to 36 pieces*

Butter Crunch Toffee

From the kitchen of P.M.

My mom made this toffee at the holidays, and now I do. I imagine many people's moms made this same toffee, as I have had it at my friends' homes. Many people I know have also remarked that they, too, use this recipe. If you have lost the recipe for this classic, search no more.

1 cup sugar
½ teaspoon salt
¼ cup water
½ cup butter
1½ cups chopped walnuts
12 ounces semisweet chocolate

1. In a medium saucepan over medium heat, combine the sugar, salt, water, and butter. Cook to a light-crack stage (285° on a candy thermometer). Test by adding a few drops to a glass of water. They should form a pliable ribbon. Remove from the heat, and add ½ cup of the chopped walnuts.
2. Mix well, and pour onto a well-greased cookie sheet or jelly roll pan. Set aside to let cool, about 20 minutes.
3. In a double boiler or metal bowl placed over a saucepan of simmering water, melt 6 ounces of the chocolate. Spread evenly on top of the cooled candy. Sprinkle with another ½ cup of the chopped walnuts. Set aside to let cool, about 20 minutes.
4. When cool, turn the candy over. In the same double boiler, melt the remaining 6 ounces of chocolate, and spread it on top of the candy. Sprinkle with the remaining ½ cup of walnuts. When the chocolate has cooled, break the toffee into pieces.

✶ *Makes 24 pieces*

Peanut Butter Fudge

From the kitchen of P.B.

This recipe sounds too simple to be good, but it really is delicious.

2 cups sugar	**Pinch of salt**
10 tablespoons milk	**1 cup chunky peanut butter**

1. In a medium saucepan over medium-high heat, combine the sugar, milk, and salt. Bring to a boil, and cook for 1 minute. Remove from the heat, and with a wooden spoon, stir in the peanut butter. Beat until smooth and thick.
2. Transfer to a buttered pan, and spread evenly. Let cool before cutting.

✶ *Makes 1 pound*

Ribbon Fantasy Fudge

From the kitchen of Amanda Line

At Christmastime this yummy, layered fudge always looks great on the cookie tray.

1½ plus 1½ cups sugar
6 plus 6 tablespoons margarine
⅓ plus ⅓ cup evaporated milk
6 ounces chocolate chips
7 ounces marshmallow cream
½ plus ½ teaspoon vanilla extract
½ cup peanut butter

1. Grease a 9 x 13-inch pan.
2. Combine 1½ cups sugar, 6 tablespoons margarine, and ⅓ cup evaporated milk. Stirring constantly, bring to a full, rolling boil. Boil for 4 minutes, stirring constantly. Remove from the heat, and stir in the chocolate chips until melted. Add half the marshmallow cream and ½ teaspoon vanilla. Beat until well blended. Pour into the prepared pan.
3. In a clean, medium saucepan over medium heat, combine the remaining 1½ cups sugar, the remaining 6 tablespoons margarine, and the remaining ⅓ cup evaporated milk. Stirring constantly, bring to a full, rolling boil. Boil for 4 minutes, stirring constantly. Remove from the heat, and stir in the peanut butter until melted. Add the remaining half of the marshmallow cream and the remaining ½ teaspoon vanilla. Beat until well blended. Spread over the chocolate layer. Cool and cut.

⁎ *Makes 3 pounds*

Tiger's Butter

From the kitchen of C.A.

There is always a long line to lick this bowl.

2 cups melted white chocolate
2 cups melted milk chocolate
1 cup smooth peanut butter

1. Butter a 12-inch square baking pan.
2. In a small bowl, beat the white chocolate and peanut butter until smooth and creamy. Add the milk chocolate, and fold two or three times to slightly incorporate.
3. Transfer the mixture to the prepared pan, and using a table knife, draw the milk chocolate through the white chocolate mixture to marbleize.
4. When set, cut into squares, and wrap each square in colored foil.

Variations:

For balls, when the mixture is just barely set, cut into small squares, and roll each square into a ball. Dip each ball into melted white, milk, or semisweet chocolate. Let the balls sit on wax paper until dry. Wrap the balls in foil, or place in colorful paper candy cups.

For molded chocolates, pour the melted mixture into plastic candy molds instead of a baking pan. Freeze for about 5 minutes. Pop the molded chocolates onto waxed paper and let sit until completely solid.

✶ *Makes 24 to 30 pieces*

8

Cakes, Pies, and Desserts

Bridge Cake (Kathy Cake)

From the kitchen of Kathy Ohling

I couldn't drink milk as a child, so my grandmother adapted this cake recipe for me. It's real name is Bridge Cake, but it's known in my family as Kathy Cake.

1½ cups flour
1 cup sugar
½ cup unsweetened baking cocoa
1 teaspoon baking soda
1 cup strong, cold coffee
1 teaspoon vanilla extract
1 egg, beaten
½ cup vegetable oil

1. Preheat the oven to 350°. Grease and flour a 9-inch square cake pan.
2. In a large bowl of an electric mixer, sift together the flour, sugar, cocoa, and baking soda. Add the coffee, vanilla, and egg, and mix well. Pour in the oil and mix well.
3. Pour the batter into the prepared cake pan, and bake for 25 to 30 minutes, or until a cake tester inserted in the center comes out clean. Top with a frosting, if desired.

✶ Makes 8 to 10 servings

Baltimore Bride's Cake

From the kitchen of Linda Kremsner

Baltimore Bride's Cake is an all-white cake that we had on special occasions and, of course, weddings. It was topped with coconut or sometimes sugared violets. This is the way my great-aunts and grandmother made it. It is a lot of work, but it's worth it—this cake still inhabits my dreams, where I can sometimes still taste it.

For the cake:

2 cups sifted cake flour
½ teaspoon salt
3 teaspoons baking powder
3 egg whites
½ pint (1 cup) heavy cream
1½ cups sugar
½ cup cold water
1 teaspoon vanilla extract
1 teaspoon pure almond extract

For the frosting:

1½ cups super-fine granulated sugar
⅓ cup water
2 egg whites
¼ teaspoon cream of tartar
¼ teaspoon salt
1 teaspoon vanilla extract

1. Preheat the oven to 350°. Grease and flour two 8-inch round cake pans, and line the bottom with greased wax paper.
2. To make the cake, sift together the flour, salt, and baking powder three times.
3. In a large bowl of an electric mixer, beat the egg whites until stiff but not dry.
4. In a separate bowl, whip the cream until stiff. Fold the whipped cream into the egg whites. Gradually beat in the sugar, and mix well. Working in small amounts, alternately add the flour mixture and cold water. Beat in the vanilla and almond extracts, and mix well.
5. Pour into the prepared pans, and bake until the cake begins to pull away from the sides of the pan and a toothpick inserted in the center comes out clean, about 30 minutes. Remove from the oven, and let cool completely in the pan on a wire rack.
6. To make the frosting, combine the sugar, water, egg whites, cream of tartar, and salt in a small metal bowl. Using a rotary beater or hand-held electric mixer, beat until thoroughly mixed. Place the bowl over a pot of simmering water, and beat constantly until the icing holds a peak, about 11 minutes. Remove from the heat, add the vanilla, and beat until cool and thick enough to spread.
7. Frost the cake, and let it sit until the frosting sets up, about 30 minutes.

✶ *Makes 10 servings*

Never-Fail Chocolate Cake

From the kitchen of Greer Carlisle

My grandmother made this Never-Fail Chocolate Cake. If you are not a baker, not to worry—neither am I. I have never had this cake fail, and it is delicious. A chocolate lover's dream. No holiday, birthday, or family get-together is complete without Babcia's ("grandmother" in Polish) chocolate cake.

2 cups all-purpose flour
2 cups granulated sugar
½ teaspoon salt
1 stick butter
1 cup water
½ cup cooking oil
4 tablespoons cocoa
½ cup buttermilk
1 teaspoon baking soda
1 teaspoon cinnamon
2 teaspoons vanilla extract
2 eggs, slightly beaten

For the icing:
1 (1-pound) box confectioners' sugar
1 stick butter
4 tablespoons cocoa
¼ cup plus 4 tablespoons milk
1 teaspoon vanilla extract
Chopped pecans (optional)

1. Preheat the oven to 350°. Grease two 8-inch round cake pans, and line the bottoms with greased wax paper.
2. Mix the flour, sugar, and salt together in a bowl.
3. Put the butter, water, oil, and cocoa in a pan, and bring to a boil. Be sure to stir continuously, so the mixture doesn't stick to the bottom of the pan. When the mixture boils, pour it into the flour/sugar/salt mixture. Add the buttermilk, baking soda, cinnamon, vanilla, and eggs.
4. Pour the batter into the prepared pans, and bake until a toothpick inserted in the center comes out clean, about 25 minutes. Remove from the oven, let cool in the pans for 10 minutes, and then transfer to a wire rack to cool completely.
5. To make the icing, put the confectioners' sugar in a medium bowl. In a small saucepan over high heat, combine the butter, cocoa, and milk, and bring to a boil. Pour the mixture over the confectioners' sugar, and add the vanilla. Stir until creamy. Spread a small amount of the frosting on the top of one cake, and top with the second cake. Cover both layers with the rest of the frosting. Sprinkle the cake with chopped pecans and serve.

✶ *Makes 10 servings*

Burnt Sugar Cake with Burnt Sugar Frosting

From the kitchen of Judie Oberheuser

I've used this recipe for years. This cake is super and very rich.

For the syrup:
1 cup sugar
1 cup boiling water

For the cake:
3 cups sifted cake flour
1 tablespoon baking powder
½ teaspoon salt
¾ cup butter, softened
1 plus ¼ cups granulated sugar
3 eggs, separated
1 teaspoon vanilla extract
¾ cup milk

For the frosting:
½ cup butter
1 (1-pound) box confectioners' sugar
2 teaspoons vanilla extract
Pecan halves (optional)

1. Preheat the oven to 350°. Grease two 9-inch round cake pans, and line the bottom with greased wax paper.
2. To make the syrup, in a large skillet over low heat, heat the sugar until melted and amber colored. Watch carefully. Remove from the heat. Carefully stir in the boiling water, and mix until the sugar is dissolved. Cool. Measure ½ cup for the cake, and reserve the rest for the frosting.
3. To make the cake, sift together the flour, baking powder, and salt.
4. In a large bowl of an electric mixer, beat the butter until creamy. Add 1 cup sugar, the egg yolks, and vanilla, and beat until light and fluffy. Beat in the ½ cup burnt sugar syrup. Add in the flour mixture alternately with the milk, beating after each addition until smooth.
5. In a clean medium bowl, beat the egg whites until foamy. Gradually add the remaining ¼ cup sugar, and continue beating until soft peaks form. Fold the egg whites into the batter until no streaks of white remain.
6. Transfer the batter to the prepared pans. Bake until a toothpick inserted in the center comes out clean and the cake springs back when touched with a fingertip, about 25 minutes. Cool in the pans for 5 minutes. Remove the cakes from the pans, pull off the paper, and transfer them to a wire rack to cool completely.
7. To make the burnt sugar frosting, beat the butter until light and fluffy in a bowl of an electric mixer. Beat in the confectioners' sugar alternately with the remaining

burnt sugar syrup and the vanilla, mixing well after each addition. Beat until the frosting is creamy and spreadable.

8. Place one cake layer on a plate or serving platter, and cover the top with a layer of frosting. Carefully place the second cake layer on top, and frost the entire cake with the remaining frosting. Garnish with pecan halves.

* *Makes 12 to 14 servings*

Coconut Walnut Cake

From the kitchen of S.B.

My husband goes crazy over this fantastic upside-down cake.

¼ cup dark corn syrup
3 tablespoons butter, melted
3 tablespoons firmly packed brown sugar
¾ cup flaked coconut
½ cup chopped walnuts
1½ cups all-purpose baking mix, such as Bisquick
½ cup granulated sugar
½ cup orange juice
1 egg
2 tablespoons cooking oil
1 teaspoon vanilla extract

1. Preheat the oven to 375°. Grease a 9-inch square baking pan.
2. In a small bowl, combine the corn syrup, butter, and brown sugar. Mix well, and spread in the bottom of the prepared pan. Sprinkle the coconut and nuts over the top.
3. In a large bowl of an electric mixer, combine the baking mix, sugar, orange juice, egg, oil, and vanilla. Beat on low speed to combine for 30 seconds. Beat on medium speed for 4 minutes or until well mixed and light.
4. Pour the batter over the nuts and coconut. Bake until a toothpick inserted in the center comes out clean, about 20 minutes. Remove from the oven, and immediately invert the cake onto a serving plate. Let cool. Tastes best served warm.

* *Makes 9 servings*

Nanny's Japanese Fruit Cake

From the kitchen of A.M.

My grandmother's signature holiday dessert was this cake. Enjoy!

For the cake:
1 pound raisins
1 plus 3 cups all-purpose flour
4 teaspoons baking powder
2 teaspoons ground cinnamon
1 teaspoon ground cloves
1 teaspoon ground nutmeg
1 cup butter
2 cups sugar
6 eggs, separated
1 cup milk
1 cup flaked coconut
1 cup chopped pecans

For the frosting:
2 cups sugar
1½ cups hot water
4 teaspoons all-purpose flour
1 lemon, peeled, seeded, and minced
2 large oranges, peeled, sectioned, and cut into bite-size pieces
1 pound flaked coconut
1 cup pecan halves
1 cup maraschino cherries, halved

1. Preheat the oven to 350 degrees. Grease and flour two 9-inch round cake pans.
2. To make the cake, dredge the raisins in 1 cup flour. Sift together the remaining 3 cups flour, baking powder, cinnamon, cloves, and nutmeg.
3. In a large bowl of an electric mixer, beat the butter until creamy. Add the sugar, and beat until light and fluffy. Add the egg yolks, and beat until smooth. Gradually mix in the flour mixture alternately with the milk. Stir in the coconut, pecans, and reserved raisins.
4. In a clean bowl, beat the egg whites until stiff peaks form. Fold into the batter, and mix until just incorporated.
5. Pour the batter into the prepared pans. Bake until a toothpick inserted in the center comes out clean, about 25 minutes. Remove the cakes from the pans, and cool on a wire rack.
6. To make the frosting, in a medium saucepan over medium heat, combine the sugar, water, flour, lemon, and oranges. Cook until thickened. Stir in the coconut, and cook for an additional 2 minutes. Let cool.
7. Spread the frosting on the cake, and decorate by alternating pecan halves and maraschino cherry halves around the top of the cake to form a pinwheel.

∗ *Makes 10 to 12 servings*

Poke Cake

From the kitchen of Carol Montague

This delicious cake idea has been around many years. Maybe some younger moms have not heard of it. Give it a try—it's easy and delicious. I prepare a festive Christmas variation using red and green Jell-O and white cake around the holidays, and it always attracts compliments. Always a huge hit with the kids, this cake is made by just combining your favorite flavor of Jell-O with a complementary flavor of cake. Some people even use instant pudding. The number of variations that other families use illustrates that my family isn't the only one who loves to play with this cake.

1 (4-ounce) package Jell-O brand gelatin (any flavor)
¾ cup hot water
1 cup cold water
1 (18.25-ounce) package cake mix (any flavor)

1. In a large bowl, dissolve the Jell-O in the hot water. Stir in the cold water and set aside, but do not refrigerate.
2. Prepare the cake mix according to instructions on the box. Pour into a greased and floured 9 x 13-inch pan, and bake until a toothpick inserted in the center comes out clean. Cool in the pan for 25 minutes.
3. With a meat fork, poke holes all over the cake. Slowly pour the warm Jell-O over the cake. Chill. Does not need frosting, but can be served with whipped topping.

✶ *Makes 10 servings*

Italian Cream Cake with Cream Cheese Frosting

From the kitchen of N.B.

I believe this old recipe came from an Italian relative. It's a wonderful cake.

For the cake:
5 eggs, separated
½ cup butter or margarine
½ cup vegetable shortening
2 cups granulated sugar
1 teaspoon baking soda
1 cup buttermilk
2 cups all-purpose flour
3 ounces flaked coconut
1 cup chopped nuts
1 teaspoon vanilla extract
1 teaspoon coconut extract

For the frosting:
1 (8-ounce) package cream cheese
½ cup butter or margarine
1 teaspoon pure almond extract
1 pound confectioners' sugar

1. Preheat the oven to 350°. Grease and flour three 9-inch round cake pans.
2. To make the cake, in a large, clean bowl of an electric mixer, beat the egg whites until stiff.
3. In a separate bowl, beat the butter and shortening until creamy. Add the sugar, and beat until light and fluffy. Add the egg yolks, one at a time, beating well after each addition.
4. In a small bowl, dissolve the baking soda into the buttermilk, and mix well. Gradually add the buttermilk mixture to the batter alternately with the flour, mixing well after each addition. Add the coconut, nuts, vanilla, and coconut extract. Fold in the reserved egg whites until just incorporated.
5. Pour 2 cups batter into each of the prepared pans. Bake until a toothpick inserted in the center comes out clean, about 25 minutes. Remove the cakes from the pans, and cool completely on a wire rack.
6. To make the frosting, beat together the cream cheese, butter, and almond extract in a large bowl of an electric mixer until creamy. Gradually beat in the confectioners' sugar, and continue beating until light and fluffy. Spread between the layers, and then frost the cake.

✶ *Makes 10 to 12 servings*

Italian Rum Pastry Cake (Cassatta)

From the kitchen of Giovanna Roy

This is my favorite cake. Talk about bringing back memories! It's the cake my family has at every holiday and special occasion. Making this cake the traditional way is very long and involved, so we usually buy it—even though it means a long ride into Boston to our favorite Italian bakery.

1 (18.25-ounce) box yellow cake mix
1 (3-ounce) box regular chocolate pudding mix
1 (3-ounce) box regular vanilla pudding mix
1 cup dark rum or Myers fruit rum
2½ cups whipping cream
1 teaspoon vanilla extract
⅓ cup sugar
Maraschino cherries, drained and halved (optional)
Chocolate sprinkles or finely chopped nuts

1. Prepare the cake according to directions on the box. Pour into two 9-inch round cake pans. Bake until a toothpick inserted in the center comes out clean, and remove from the pans to cool completely on a wire rack.
2. Prepare the chocolate and vanilla puddings separately, according to the directions on the boxes. Set aside to cool.
3. With a large knife with a serrated edge, carefully cut the cooled cakes in half, making four layers. Soak the cut edge of each layer in about ¼ cup rum. Do not oversoak. Refrigerate.
4. When the pudding has cooled, place one layer of the cake on a serving plate with the rum side up. Spread the chocolate pudding over the top, and cover with a layer of the cake, rum side down. On a separate plate, repeat with the remaining two cake layers and the vanilla pudding. Cover and refrigerate the cakes.
5. In a large bowl of an electric mixer, whip the cream until stiff, gradually adding the vanilla and sugar. Spread the whipped cream on top of the chocolate-filled layers. Sprinkle the cherries on top of the whipped cream. Carefully place the remaining layers (those filled with the vanilla pudding) on top, and use the remaining whipped cream to cover the top and sides of the cake.
6. Decorate with pastry flowers, candied flowers, chocolate sprinkles, or nuts, if desired.

∗ *Makes 12 to 14 servings*

Poppy Seed Cake

From the kitchen of Pamela Bennett

I have served this cake for years at showers, parties, and even funerals. It is a favorite. It can be prepared with or without the glaze; both versions are delicious.

For the cake:

1 (18.25-ounce) box white or yellow cake mix
1 (3-ounce) instant lemon pudding mix
4 tablespoons poppy seeds
1 cup water
½ cup cooking oil
1 teaspoon pure almond extract
4 eggs

For the glaze:

2 cups confectioners' sugar
Juice and grated zest of 2 lemons
2 tablespoons butter

1. Preheat the oven to 350°. Spray a 10-inch Bundt cake pan with nonstick cooking spray, and coat with a cinnamon-sugar mixture.
2. To make the cake, in a large bowl of an electric mixer, combine the cake mix, pudding mix, and poppy seeds. Add the water, oil, and almond extract. Mix well. Add the eggs, one at a time, beating well after each addition.
3. Transfer to the prepared baking pan, and bake until a toothpick inserted in the center comes out clean, about 45 minutes. Let the cake cool in the pan for 15 minutes. Remove from the pan, and transfer to a wire rack to cool completely.
4. To make the glaze, in a heavy saucepan over medium heat, combine the sugar, lemon juice, lemon zest, and butter. Bring to a boil, and cook for 1 minute. Remove from the heat, and drizzle the glaze over the top of the cake.

✶ *Makes 10 servings*

"Hog-Killing" Cake

From the kitchen of Kerri Kerr

When friends came together for "hog-killing day," they enjoyed this cake. Laura Ingalls Wilder talks about her family's hog-killing day in one of our favorite books, Little House in the Big Woods. *I've made the cake simpler by using boxed cake mix.*

For the cake:

1 (18.25-ounce) box all-butter cake mix
4 large eggs
¼ cup vegetable oil
1 (11-ounce) can mandarin oranges with juice
1 cup black walnuts

For the frosting:

4 ounces butter (or margarine), softened
1 (8-ounce) package cream cheese, softened
1 (8-ounce) can crushed pineapple, drained
3 cups confectioners' sugar

1. Preheat the oven to 350°.
2. To make the cake, in a medium bowl, combine the cake mix, eggs, and vegetable oil. Stir in the undrained mandarin oranges and walnuts.
3. Pour the batter into two 9-inch round cake pans. Bake for 25 minutes. Transfer to a wire rack to cool.
4. To make the frosting, in a small bowl, mix the butter, cream cheese, pineapple, and sugar. Chill the frosting in the refrigerator for 30 minutes to allow it to firm up. Using a spatula or knife, spread the frosting over the cake.

✶ *Makes 12 servings*

One-Pan Chocolate Cake

From the kitchen of Judie Oberheuser

We had this 1950s classic every Saturday night. Sometimes my mom would dust it with powdered sugar, and sometimes she would frost it with chocolate frosting. Be careful not to overstir the batter—if you do, the cake will take on the color of licorice.

1½ cups all-purpose flour
1 cup sugar
3 tablespoons unsweetened cocoa powder
1 teaspoon baking soda
½ teaspoon salt
6 tablespoons salad oil
1 tablespoon vinegar
1 teaspoon vanilla extract
1 cup chilled water

1. Preheat the oven to 350°.
2. Sift together flour, sugar, cocoa, baking soda, and salt, and place in a nonstick, ungreased 9-inch square baking pan. Make three depressions in the flour mixture. Pour the oil in one, vinegar in another, and vanilla in the third. Pour the water over all, and stir with a fork just until lumps are gone.
3. Bake until a toothpick inserted in the center comes out clean, about 30 minutes. Let cool completely in the pan.
4. Place a paper doily on the cake, and sprinkle lightly with powdered sugar. Remove the doily and serve. (The cake may also be frosted with a chocolate frosting.)

✶ *Makes 8 servings*

Pound Cake

From the kitchen of C.G.

1 cup butter or margarine
1⅔ cups sugar
5 eggs
1 teaspoon vanilla extract
2 cups all-purpose flour

1. Preheat the oven to 350°. Grease and flour a 9 x 5-inch loaf pan.
2. Beat the butter in a large bowl of an electric mixer until creamy. Mix in the sugar, and beat until light and fluffy. Add the eggs, one at a time, beating well after each addition. Stir in the vanilla and flour, and mix well.
3. Transfer to the prepared pan, and bake until a toothpick inserted in the center comes out clean, about 1 hour.

Variation: Use lemon extract instead of vanilla, and add a few drops of yellow food coloring to give it a twist.

∗ *Makes 8 servings*

Bubbe's Jewish Apple Cake

From the kitchen of Jenny Saltiel

My great-grandmother Sarah was a wonderful cook from Austria who never used a recipe, even when she baked. Instead, she would improvise, adding whatever ingredients struck her fancy. One of her daughter's favorite desserts was a simple cake made with crisp, tart apples and sweet, golden crust that filled their home with an aroma of cinnamon and butter. When her daughter—my grandmother—got married, she watched Sarah make it and took notes so that she could bake this treat for her own family. My mother likes telling me this story whenever she makes this dessert. It will always be my ultimate comfort food.

This cake is the perfect end to any holiday meal. It can be served warm with vanilla bean ice cream or alone at room temperature.

2 eggs
1 cup sugar
½ cup vegetable oil
½ teaspoon vanilla extract
1 teaspoon baking powder
1½ cups all-purpose flour
5 Granny Smith apples, peeled and thinly sliced
1 tablespoon cinnamon sugar for sprinkling
1 tablespoon butter

1. Preheat the oven to 350°. Grease and flour an 8-inch square baking pan.
2. In a medium bowl, combine the eggs, sugar, oil, vanilla, baking powder, and flour. Mix well.
3. Transfer half of the mixture into the prepared pan. Place the sliced apples in an even layer on top of the dough. Sprinkle the cinnamon sugar on top of the apples, and dot with the butter. Spoon the remaining half of the batter on top of the apples. Do not completely cover the apples.
4. Bake until light to golden brown, about 1 hour. Serve warm, or let cool in the pan on a wire rack.

∗ *Makes 6 to 8 servings*

Grandma Rose's Applesauce Cake

From the kitchen of N.D.

Here's one from the kitchen of my grandmother, Rose Davis Welton. It always makes me think of fall and apple harvest time when I smell it baking. We serve it with cream cheese icing or just dusted with powdered sugar.

3/4 cup butter
1 1/2 cups sugar
2 eggs
2 1/2 cups applesauce
3 teaspoons baking soda
3 cups all-purpose flour
1 1/2 teaspoons salt
1 teaspoon ground nutmeg
1 teaspoon ground cinnamon
1 cup raisins
1/2 cup chopped walnuts

1. Preheat the oven to 350°. Grease and flour a 9 x 13-inch pan.
2. In a large bowl of an electric mixer, beat the butter until smooth. Add the sugar, and beat until light and fluffy. Add the eggs, one at a time, beating well after each addition. Stir in the applesauce.
3. Sift together the baking soda, flour, salt, nutmeg, and cinnamon. Add to the batter, and mix well. Stir in the raisins and nuts.
4. Pour the batter into the prepared pan, and bake until a toothpick inserted in the center comes out clean, about 45 to 50 minutes. Cool completely in the pan.

✶ *Makes 16 servings*

Chocolate Chip Date Nut Cake

From the kitchen of Elizabeth Lavalle

I recently passed this recipe on to my granddaughter. It comes from my mother's sister, Ethel, who, at 102 years young, continues to correspond with me. I was so happy to give this recipe to my granddaughter, because it's also her mother's and her aunt's favorite cake. I hope others will enjoy it, too.

For the cake:

1 cup chopped dates (packed)
1 cup boiling water
½ cup shortening
1 cup granulated sugar
1 egg
1 teaspoon vanilla extract
¼ teaspoon salt
1⅔ cups all-purpose flour
1 teaspoon baking soda
½ cup walnuts
6 ounces chocolate chips

For the topping:

¾ cup brown sugar
4 tablespoons butter
½ cup chopped nuts
4 ounces chocolate chips

1. Preheat the oven to 350°. Grease and flour a 9 x 13-inch pan.
2. Add the dates to the water, and cool until the mixture is warm.
3. In a large bowl of an electric mixer, beat together the shortening and sugar until light and fluffy. Add the egg and vanilla, and mix well. Add the date mixture, and mix well. Add the salt, flour, and baking soda, and mix. Add the chocolate chips and nuts, and pour into the prepared pan.
4. For the topping, work the brown sugar and butter together with your hands until the mixture resembles a fine meal. Mix in the nuts and chocolate chips. Sprinkle the topping over the cake batter, and bake 35 to 40 minutes.

∗ *Makes 8 to 10 servings*

Grandmother's Strawberry Shortcake

From the kitchen of Gloria DelCambre

My grandmother made this for my birthday cake the year I turned 10 (which was in 1942). I was so honored. Using water instead of milk makes the biscuits lighter and fluffier.

2 cups all-purpose flour
2 teaspoons baking powder
1 teaspoon salt
3 tablespoons sugar
¼ cup solid vegetable shortening, cut into pieces
1 egg, beaten
⅓ cup water
1 tablespoon butter, melted
4 cups sliced strawberries, sweetened
Whipped cream

1. Preheat the oven to 450°.
2. In the bowl of a food processor fitted with the stainless steel blade, place the flour, baking powder, salt, and sugar. Pulse two or three times to blend. Add the shortening, and process to form a coarse meal.
3. Transfer to a large bowl, and make a well in the center of the batter. Pour the egg and water into the well, and using a fork, pull the egg mixture through the flour. If necessary, add more water to make the dough more manageable. Pat the dough into a ball, and turn onto a lightly floured surface.
4. Pat the dough into a ½-inch-thick disk. Dip a 3-inch biscuit cutter in flour, and cut the dough into biscuits. Place the biscuits one inch apart on a baking sheet. Brush with the melted butter, and bake until golden brown, about 12 to 15 minutes.
5. Split the hot shortcakes, and fill with sweetened strawberries and whipped cream.

∗ *Makes 8 to 10 servings*

My Mom's Decorator Frosting

From the kitchen of Julia Schrenker

My mom's recipe is ideal for making roses and other designs. But this also produces an extremely smooth frosting when used for the basic icing—just like bakeries make. But be sure when piping that the mixture isn't too runny, or your shapes won't hold. I remember being very happy to eat my mother's "practice" work.

1 cup solid vegetable shortening
2 tablespoons butter
¼ cup milk
1 teaspoon vanilla extract
1 (2-pound) bag confectioners' sugar
1 egg white

1. In a large bowl of an electric mixer, beat the shortening and butter until creamy. Add the milk and vanilla, and mix well. Gradually beat in the sugar until just smooth. If the mixture is too stiff, add more milk, no more than a teaspoon at a time. If it gets too soft, add more sugar a small amount at a time. The frosting should be stiff enough to hold some peaks. Add the egg white, and beat again until stiff.
2. Transfer the frosting to a pastry bag, and pipe into desired designs.

✶ *Makes 1 quart frosting*

Great Aunt Helen's Peach Thing

From the kitchen of Linda Kremsner

This dessert is quick, good, and not for the faint of heart or those worried about cholesterol. My Aunt Helen used to bake her own cake from scratch and cook down the peaches with cornstarch and sugar. Not me. I make mine in 20 minutes; hers took all day.

2 (8-ounce) packages cream cheese, room temperature
1 angel food cake (bought or baked)
3 cups canned peach pie filling
1 pint heavy cream, whipped

1. In a bowl of an electric mixer, beat the cream cheese until softened.
2. Break or cut the cake into bite-size pieces. With a knife, lightly coat each piece of cake with the cream cheese.
3. Place in a large serving bowl. Stir in the peaches and whipped cream, and mix well. Serve immediately or refrigerate until served.

✶ *Makes 10 to 12 servings*

Ma-Ma's No-Bake Fruitcake

From the kitchen of A.M.

My maternal grandmother (whom we called "Ma-Ma") was famous for this no-bake fruitcake. The following is straight from her handwritten notes, found hidden in a tin in her pantry after she passed away.

½ teaspoon salt
½ teaspoon ground cloves
½ teaspoon allspice
1½ cups mixed candied fruit
½ cup candied cherries
1 teaspoon ground cinnamon
½ teaspoon ground nutmeg
2 cups chopped pecans
1 cup glazed pineapple, chopped
½ cup golden raisins
2 cups miniature marshmallows
2 cups heavy cream
1 pound graham crackers, crushed

1. In a large bowl, combine the salt, cloves, allspice, candied fruit, cherries, cinnamon, nutmeg, pecans, pineapple, raisins, and marshmallows. Mix well.
2. In a separate bowl, whip the cream until stiff. Stir the fruit mixture into the cream. Using a wooden spoon, gradually stir in the graham cracker crumbs, and mix well.
3. Transfer to a graham cracker box lined with foil, and refrigerate until chilled. Cut into thin slices to serve.

✶ *Makes 14 servings*

Positively Pearable Pie

From the kitchen of Alysia Korelc

When I was growing up, we lived on a cul-de-sac where all the families had children within the same age group. We were a close-knit community, and we enjoyed block parties around our pool or a neighbor's and were even known to block off the street to gather the camp stoves at the end of the cul-de-sac. One day, one of the dads was visiting, and we were all talking about pie. He challenged me to make a pear pie, because I made the mistake of saying I had never heard of such a thing. So this is what I produced, and, much to my own surprise, everyone loved it. I was barely 16 at the time. I still make this pie every now and then.

2 (10- to 11-inch) unbaked piecrusts (store-bought or homemade)
2 (28-ounce) cans pear halves, drained
½ cup unsalted butter, cut into small cubes
Juice of 1 lemon
1 cup dark brown sugar
¼ teaspoon ground cinnamon
1 egg white, beaten

1. Preheat the oven to 400°.
2. Place 1 crust into a deep-dish, 9-inch pie pan, and lightly prick the bottom with a fork. Heap the drained pear halves into the pie shell, and dot generously with half the cubed butter. Evenly sprinkle the pears with the lemon juice, brown sugar, and cinnamon. Dot with the remaining butter.
3. Carefully lay the second crust over the pears. Trim, crimp, and seal the edges of the crust.
4. Cut two or three leaf shapes and a stem out of scraps of crust, and carefully lay them over the top of the crust. With a small sharp knife, cut a few small slits into the crust, and brush the entire crust with the beaten egg white.
5. Bake until the crust is golden brown, about 20 to 30 minutes. Let cool on a pie rack for a few minutes. Serve warm with French vanilla ice cream or cooled with freshly whipped cream.

∗ *Makes 6 to 8 servings*

My Grandmother's Lemon Meringue Pie

From the kitchen of P.N.

1 (9-inch) prebaked piecrust, fresh or frozen

For the filling:

1¼ cups sugar
6 tablespoons cornstarch
2 cups water
3 eggs, separated
⅓ cup lemon juice
3 tablespoons butter
1½ teaspoons lemon extract
2 teaspoons vinegar

For the meringue:

1 tablespoon cornstarch
2 tablespoons water
½ cup boiling water
1 teaspoon vanilla extract
Pinch of salt
6 tablespoons sugar

1. Preheat the oven to 400°.
2. To make the filling, in a saucepan over medium heat, combine the sugar, cornstarch, and water. Bring to a boil, and cook for 2 minutes. Remove from the heat.
3. In a small bowl, beat the egg yolks with the lemon juice. Gradually add half of the hot sugar mixture into the yolks. Return the tempered egg yolks to the saucepan. Set the pan back on the heat, and boil, stirring constantly until thick, about 2 minutes. Blend in the butter, lemon extract, and vinegar. Mix well. Pour into the baked piecrust.
4. To make the meringue, combine the cornstarch and cold water in a saucepan over low heat. Add the boiling water, and cook until thick and clear. Let cool.
5. Meanwhile, in a large bowl of an electric mixer, beat the egg whites until thick and stiff but not dry. Gradually add in the sugar, salt, and vanilla. Beat on high, and gradually add in the cooled mixture.
6. Using a spoonful at a time and starting at the edges of the pie, place the meringue over the pie filling. Moving toward the center last, cover the filling completely with the meringue. Using the back of the spoon, swirl the meringue into peaks.
7. Bake until light brown, about 8 to 10 minutes. Watch carefully to prevent burning.

∗ *Makes 8 servings*

Coconut Cream Pie

From the kitchen of Pamela Moore

When I was first married (over 20 years ago), I wanted to surprise my husband by making his favorite pie. I have tweaked the recipe over the years, and it's become a family tradition for me to bring it to all gatherings. It has also been the top seller at many bake sales. I usually triple this recipe and take two pies to the potluck or gathering and leave one at home for my husband. He still eats a couple of pieces at the gathering anyway.

I'm not even a sweet eater, but I do like the taste of this pie. I use frozen piecrusts when making this as well; the filling tastes so good, no one ever notices.

1 (9-inch) prebaked piecrust

For the filling:

¾ cup sugar
⅓ cup all-purpose flour
¼ teaspoon salt
2 cups milk
3 egg yolks, beaten
2 tablespoons butter
1 teaspoon vanilla extract
2 cups shredded coconut plus 2 tablespoons for topping

For the meringue:

¼ teaspoon cream of tartar
3 egg whites
2 tablespoons sugar

1. To make the filling, in a heavy saucepan, combine the sugar, flour, and salt, and slowly whisk in the milk. Set the pan over medium heat. Stirring constantly, bring to a full boil. Let boil for 2 minutes, stirring constantly. Remove from the heat, and whisk a small amount of the hot mixture into the egg yolks. Pour the egg mixture back into the milk mixture, and return to the heat. Stirring constantly, bring to a simmer, and cook for 2 minutes more. Remove from the heat.
2. If necessary, pour through a strainer or sieve to remove any lumps, and return to the pan. Stir in the butter, vanilla, and coconut. Mix well. Pour into the baked piecrust, and let cool.
3. Preheat the oven to 425°.
4. To make the meringue, in a clean bowl of an electric mixer, add the cream of tartar to the egg whites, and beat until stiff. When the egg whites are whipped, slowly beat in the sugar.
5. Spoon the meringue over the custard, and sprinkle with the coconut. Bake in the oven, watching carefully, until the meringue is light brown and the coconut is toasted, about 5 minutes.

⁎ *Makes 6 to 8 servings*

Mom's Pumpkin Pie

From the kitchen of Giovanna Roy

This recipe has been in my family forever. One year, I got it in my head to search for the perfect pumpkin pie recipe. I figured that this old-fashioned one must have been improved many times over since its inception. I scoured my cookbooks, making one after the other—using heavy cream instead of evaporated milk and less or more exotic spices. And in the end, I found out that I love my mom's version the best. I used to turn my nose up at the evaporated milk, but the truth is that it consistently makes a nice, silky pie, and the spices in this recipe are perfectly balanced. Some things can't be improved on.

1 cup sugar
1½ teaspoons ground cinnamon
½ teaspoon ground cloves
½ teaspoon ground allspice
½ teaspoon ground nutmeg
½ teaspoon ground ginger
½ teaspoon salt
1 (14-ounce) can pumpkin puree
1 (5-ounce) can evaporated milk
2 eggs
1 (9-inch) unbaked piecrust

1. Preheat the oven to 425°.
2. In a small bowl, whisk together the sugar, cinnamon, cloves, allspice, nutmeg, ginger, and salt.
3. In a large bowl, mix the pumpkin, evaporated milk, and eggs until blended. Add the sugar mixture, and mix again.
4. Pour the mixture into the crust, and bake for 15 minutes. Reduce the heat to 350°, and bake until the filling looks dull and a knife inserted half way between the edge and the center of the pie comes out clean, about 40 minutes.

✶ *Makes 8 servings*

Southern Pecan Pie

From the kitchen of Kelly M.

Although this recipe is very simple, it's the best pecan pie I've ever had. I hope you agree.

3 eggs
⅔ cup sugar
Dash of salt
1 cup dark corn syrup
⅓ cup butter or margarine, melted
1 cup pecan halves
1 (9-inch) unbaked piecrust

1. Preheat the oven to 350°.
2. In a large bowl of an electric mixer, beat the eggs until frothy. Add the sugar, salt, syrup, and melted butter. Mix well. Stir in the pecans.
3. Pour the mixture into the piecrust. Bake until a knife inserted halfway between the center and edge comes out clean, about 50 minutes. Transfer to a wire rack to cool. Serve with whipped cream or vanilla ice cream.

✶ *Makes 8 servings*

Candy Apple Pie

From the kitchen of Sherry Knackstept

For the crust:

3 tablespoons sugar
1½ cups graham cracker crumbs
½ teaspoon ground cinnamon
⅓ cup butter, melted

For the filling:

5 Granny Smith apples, peeled and sliced
½ cup firmly packed brown sugar
¼ teaspoon salt
5 tablespoons butter

For the cream cheese topping:

1 (8-ounce) package cream cheese, softened
1 teaspoon lemon juice
¼ cup granulated sugar
1 teaspoon vanilla extract

For the topping:

¾ cup caramel ice cream topping
¼ cup chopped pecans

1. Preheat the oven to 370°.
2. In a large bowl, combine the sugar, graham cracker crumbs, cinnamon, and melted butter. Mix well, and evenly press into a 9-inch pie pan. Bake for 16 minutes. Cool on a wire rack.
3. For the filling, in a medium saucepan over medium heat, combine the apples, brown sugar, salt, and butter. Stirring occasionally, cook until the apples begin to soften, about 10 to 15 minutes. Pour into the crust.
4. For the cream cheese topping, combine the cream cheese, lemon juice, sugar, and vanilla in a bowl. Mix well.
5. Spread the cream cheese topping evenly over the apples. Bake until a golden brown crust forms, about 30 minutes. Transfer the pie to a wire rack to cool.
6. Top with the caramel sauce and pecans.

∗ *Makes 8 to 10 servings*

Blueberry Tart with Cream Cheese Crust and Streusel Topping

From the kitchen of Elaine Kurschner

For the crust:

1 cup all-purpose flour plus ¼ cup for rolling out
½ tablespoon sugar
⅛ teaspoon salt
3 ounces cream cheese, softened
½ cup unsalted butter, cold and cut into small pieces

For the filling:

3½ to 4 cups blueberries, washed, picked over, and well-drained
1 cup granulated sugar
3 tablespoons tapioca

For the topping:

1 cup brown sugar
½ cup all-purpose flour
½ cup butter
1 teaspoon ground cinnamon

1. In the bowl of a food processor fitted with the stainless steel blade, combine the flour, sugar, and salt. Pulse two or three times to blend. Add the cream cheese, and process until well mixed. Add the butter, and process until the mixture resembles coarse meal.
2. Transfer to a sheet of plastic wrap, form into a ball, wrap, and chill for one hour.
3. Preheat the oven to 350°.
4. On a lightly floured surface, roll out the dough into a circle large enough to fit a 9-inch pie or tart pan. Transfer the dough to the pie pan, and crimp the edges. Chill until ready to fill.
5. For the filling, combine the blueberries, sugar, and tapioca in a bowl. Mix well. Transfer to the pie shell.
6. For the topping, in the clean bowl of a food processor, combine the brown sugar, flour, butter, and cinnamon. Process until crumbly. Sprinkle on top of the blueberries.
7. Bake until the top and crust are brown and the filling is bubbly and thickened, about 40 minutes.

* *Makes 8 servings*

Fruit Tarts

From the kitchen of Francine McCarthy

For a while, I belonged to an email recipe swap consisting of 13 women. We called ourselves "The Baker's Dozen." The recipe swap eventually ended, but we still keep in touch and know whom to call if a good recipe is needed. This is one of the recipes I received as part of that group.

These very simple tarts may be made in miniature, gem-sized muffin tins for finger desserts, in individual tart pans, or in a large tart pan. The heat from the shell and preserves is all that's needed to soften the fresh fruits. My favorite combinations are seedless strawberry preserves with fresh strawberry slices, blueberry preserves with fresh blueberries, and seedless raspberry preserves with fresh raspberries. I serve this with unsweetened whipped cream. We're used to having it that way and prefer the natural, sugar-free flavor.

3 ounces cream cheese, softened
½ cup butter, softened
1 cup all-purpose flour
½ teaspoon salt
8 tablespoons Polaner All-Fruit or Smucker's Natural Preserves
1 pint fresh berries

1. In the bowl of a food processor, combine the cream cheese, butter, flour, and salt. Process until the mixture resembles coarse meal. Transfer to a sheet of plastic wrap, form into a ball, wrap, and chill for 1 hour.
2. Preheat the oven to 350°.
3. Press the dough into pan(s), and bake for 10 minutes. Fill each tart with preserves. Return to the oven, and continue baking until the preserves are just bubbling, about 5 minutes more. Remove immediately, and top with fresh berries.

✶ *Makes 8 servings*

Rhubarb Crisp

From the kitchen of H.B.

I'm not an old cook. I'm not a child of an old cook either; my mother is 50 and never was much of a cook. But I love to cook, and I love old-style rhubarb desserts. I have a million rhubarb recipes—this one is for a good old-fashioned rhubarb crisp, the kind that is perfect served with vanilla ice cream.

6 cups diced rhubarb
2 cups sugar
1½ cups all-purpose flour
½ cup butter, softened
½ teaspoon salt

1. Preheat the oven to 350°. Grease a 9 x 13-inch pan.
2. Evenly spread the rhubarb in the prepared pan.
3. In a bowl of a food processor, combine the sugar, flour, butter, and salt. Process until the mixture resembles peas.
4. Evenly spread the crumb mixture over the rhubarb. Bake until lightly browned and rhubarb is bubbling, about 40 minutes.

✶ *Makes 8 servings*

Blackberry Cobbler

From the kitchen of Donna Corrine Bailey

My maternal grandmother used to make this blackberry cobbler, and my mother has made it every summer for as long as I can remember. She and her father would go out to pick blackberries, and the result was always a few pies and many, many cobblers. She says that as long as she can remember her mother made this, and that it was the very first thing she baked by herself for company. I remember watching with absolute wonder as the berries went from the top of this cobbler through to the bottom. I'm delighted that I'll get to pass this along to a fourth generation of women when it comes time for my daughter to learn how to bake.

1 cup flour
1 plus ½ cups sugar plus some for sprinkling
¼ teaspoon salt
2 teaspoons baking powder
¼ cup butter
1 egg, slightly beaten
½ cup milk
2 cups blackberries
1 cup boiling water
Cinnamon (optional)

1. Preheat the oven to 350°. Grease a 9-inch square pan.
2. In a small bowl, sift the flour, 1 cup sugar, salt, and baking powder. In a medium bowl, cream the butter and the remaining ½ cup sugar together. Stir in the egg, flour mixture, and milk. The batter should be thick and lumpy.
3. Pour the batter into the prepared pan. Scatter the berries on top of the batter, and sprinkle sugar and cinnamon (optional) over them. Carefully pour the boiling water over the berries and sugar. The berries will sink through the batter. Bake for 45 minutes or until the top is golden brown.

✶ *Makes 8 servings*

Grandma Patterson's Apple Crisp

From the kitchen of B.E.

This recipe is very special. I have the original recipe card that Grandma Edith wrote herself. She was always experimenting with recipes to make them her own. There was nothing like her apple crisp. We just can't make it taste like she did. But I continue to try. One secret she had was that she always used a combination of different varieties of apples—it made the flavor that much more special.

1 cup all-purpose flour
1 teaspoon baking powder
½ teaspoon salt
3 tablespoons butter
1 egg, lightly beaten
8 to 9 apples, peeled and sliced

For the cinnamon-sugar:
½ cup sugar
1 teaspoon ground cinnamon

For sugar-flour topping:
½ cup sugar
½ cup flour

1. Preheat the oven to 350°. Grease a 9-inch square pan.
2. Sift together the flour, baking powder, and salt into the bowl of a food processor. Add the butter, and process until the mixture resembles coarse meal.
3. Transfer to a bowl, and mix in the egg until just blended. Pat the dough into the prepared pan.
4. To make the cinnamon-sugar, combine the sugar and cinnamon in a small bowl. Mix well.
5. To make the sugar-flour topping, in a separate bowl, combine the sugar and flour, and mix well.
6. Place half of the apple slices on top of the dough in the pan. Sprinkle with the cinnamon-sugar mixture. Cover with the remaining apples. Sprinkle the sugar-flour mixture on top of the apples. Bake until the apples are tender to the point of a fork, about 35 to 45 minutes.

✶ *Makes 8 servings*

Stovetop Chocolate Pudding

From the kitchen of Marsha Gillett

I've made this recipe for a long time, mainly because it reminds me of simple home comfort. This pudding is very, very chocolatey and rich. Pure heaven, and it can be prepared in 45 minutes or less.

½ cup sugar
2 tablespoons cornstarch
Pinch of salt
1⅓ cups whole milk
1 large egg yolk
4 ounces fine-quality, bittersweet chocolate, chopped
1 tablespoon unsalted butter
¼ teaspoon vanilla extract

1. In a heavy saucepan whisk together the sugar, cornstarch, and salt. Whisk in the milk, egg yolk, and chocolate. Set over medium heat, and bring to a boil, stirring constantly. Boil for 1 minute, stirring constantly. Remove from heat, and whisk in the butter and vanilla. Mix well.
2. Divide the pudding between two 8-ounce ramekins. Cover with plastic wrap, and set in the freezer for 30 minutes to chill.

∗ *Makes 2 servings*

Microwave Chocolate Pudding

From the kitchen of Giovanna Roy

Here is my microwave version of the classic chocolate pudding. Of course, you can make it on the stove, too, but you have to watch it carefully. I tend to get sidetracked around my house, so the microwave works perfectly; this way, I no longer have scorched pans. I usually double this recipe, because four servings don't last very long around my house—oftentimes the pudding doesn't even get cold before it's gone.

⅓ cup sugar
⅓ cup unsweetened cocoa powder
3 tablespoons cornstarch
Pinch of salt
2 cups milk
1 teaspoon vanilla extract (optional)

1. In a microwave bowl, combine the sugar, cocoa, cornstarch, and salt. In a steady stream, slowly whisk in the milk. Mix well.
2. Microwave on high for 5 minutes and stir. Continue to microwave 3 minutes at a time, stirring after each time, until the pudding is very thick.
3. Stir in the vanilla, and either pour into individual serving dishes or into a large bowl. Refrigerate until cold.

✶ *Makes 4 servings*

Vanilla Pudding

From the kitchen of G.W.

My grandmother learned how to make this pudding from her grandmother. There aren't too many good "from scratch" pudding recipes out there, but this is one that I treasure.

2 cups sugar
3 tablespoons all-purpose flour
4 eggs
1½ cups milk
2 teaspoons vanilla extract

1. In a heavy saucepan, combine the sugar and flour. Stir in the eggs, one at a time, mixing well after each addition. Slowly stir in the milk, and set over medium heat. Cook, stirring constantly, until thickened, about 3 to 4 minutes. Remove the pan from the heat.
2. Stir in the vanilla. Transfer to serving bowls, and refrigerate to chill.

Variations:
For chocolate pudding, stir in ½ cup unsweetened cocoa powder with the vanilla.

For orange pudding, add 1 can of mandarin oranges, drained, before chilling.

For butterscotch pudding, stir in 1 cup butterscotch morsels while cooking.

For banana pudding, layer vanilla wafer cookies in the bottom of a 9 x 13-inch pan. Place a layer of ripe banana slices over the cookies, and pour warm pudding over the bananas. Cover and refrigerate overnight. Garnish with banana slices and whipped cream.

✶ *Makes 6 servings*

Menehune Bread Pudding

From the kitchen of Sassy E. Daniels

My husband's grandparents were Hawaiian, and this bread pudding comes from them. It's simple and delicious.

4 eggs, beaten
1 cup firmly packed brown sugar
½ cup melted butter
2 tablespoons all-purpose flour
1 (15-ounce) can crushed pineapple in juice or pineapple chunks
6 slices stale bread, cubed or torn

1. Preheat the oven to 350°. Butter a casserole dish.
2. In a large bowl, combine the eggs, sugar, butter, flour, pineapple with its juice, and bread cubes. Mix well.
3. Pour the mixture into the prepared dish. Bake until a knife inserted in the center comes out clean, about 1 hour.

✶ *Makes 8 servings*

Mom's Biscuit Pudding

From the kitchen of J.M.

Growing up, my sister and I didn't know too much about using cinnamon. Mom always liked to use nutmeg on her bread pudding; and she didn't make cinnamon toast—she made "pie toast," with nutmeg, sugar, and butter. We both still fix her pudding this way even now, without a whiff of cinnamon.

1 (10-count package) refrigerator biscuits
1 cup sugar
Dash of salt
4 cups milk
2 eggs, beaten
¼ cup butter, cut into thin slices
¼ teaspoon ground nutmeg

1. Bake the biscuits according to directions on the package. Cool and break into small pieces.
2. Preheat the oven to 375°. Butter a 9 x 13-inch cake pan.
3. In a large bowl, beat together the sugar, salt, milk, and eggs. Stir in the biscuit pieces, and mix well.
4. Pour the mixture into the prepared pan. Cover the mixture with butter slices, and sprinkle nutmeg on top. Bake until a knife inserted in the center comes out clean, about 1 hour.

✶ *Makes 8 servings*

Edwards Family Traditional Date Pudding

From the kitchen of A.M.

1 cup granulated sugar
1 scant cup all-purpose flour
Dash of salt
1 teaspoon baking powder
½ cup whole milk
1 plus 1 tablespoons butter
½ cup chopped pitted dates
½ cup chopped pecans
1¾ cups firmly packed brown sugar
1 teaspoon vanilla extract
1½ cups very hot water
Whipped cream

1. Preheat the oven to 400°. Grease an 8-inch square baking dish.
2. In a large bowl of an electric mixer, combine the granulated sugar, flour, salt, baking powder, milk, and 1 tablespoon butter. Beat until smooth. Stir in the dates and pecans, and mix well. Transfer to the prepared dish.
3. In a separate large bowl, combine the brown sugar, the remaining 1 tablespoon butter, vanilla, and hot water. Carefully pour the mixture over the batter. During baking, the flour mixture will rise up through the syrup. Bake until a toothpick inserted in the center comes out clean, about 30 to 40 minutes. Remove from the oven, and let cool on a wire rack. When cool, cut into thin slices. Top each serving with a dollop of whipped cream.

✶ *Makes 8 servings*

Plum Pudding

From the kitchen of Gloria DelCambre

For my family, Christmas has a special accent on festive foods and old-fashioned recipes. It's a time of good cheer, and food has been a large part of our holiday celebrations. This wonderful old plum pudding recipe was handed down to my friend Ruth by her grandmother Mag. We've since adopted it into our family, and now it's one of our holiday staples.

For the batter:

1¼ cup raisins
1 cup currants
2 cups sweet wine (such as white Zinfandel)
1 cup pitted, chopped prunes
½ cup warm water
1 cup citron, chopped
1 cup all-purpose flour
1 cup fresh bread crumbs
1½ cups ground beef suet*
4 eggs, beaten
½ cup whiskey
½ teaspoon ground cinnamon
½ teaspoon ground nutmeg
2 teaspoons sugar

For the hard sauce:

½ cup butter or margarine
1 cup sugar
1 tablespoon vanilla extract

To serve:

¼ cup plus 1 tablespoon whiskey
1 sugar cube

1. Heavily butter a 1½-quart mold or soufflé dish.
2. In a small bowl, combine the raisins, currants, and sweet wine, and soak overnight. In a separate bowl, combine the prunes with the warm water, and soak overnight. Next day, drain the fruits.
3. In the bowl of a food processor or using a meat grinder, combine the raisins, currants, prunes, and citron. Process until finely ground. For the batter, in a large bowl, using a wooden spoon, mix the flour, bread crumbs, suet, ground fruit, eggs, whiskey, cinnamon, nutmeg, and sugar. Mix well.

*Beef suet (hard fat from the kidney and loin areas of beef) is available from butchers. It is the traditional fat used in English plum pudding and most other steamed puddings. While the thought of using it may be off-putting to the modern cook, it adds a richness to the pudding that cannot be achieved by substituting other shortenings or fats. You absolutely cannot taste it in the finished product.

4. Spoon the batter into the prepared mold. In the bottom of a large pot, place two inches of water, and set a rack in the water. Set the mold on top of the rack inside the pot, and cover the pot with a lid. Bring the water to a boil, and reduce the heat so that the water is just simmering. Cook over the simmering water until a toothpick inserted in the center of the pudding comes out clean, about 3 hours. The top of the pudding should be dull and firm to the touch. Remove the pudding from the stove, and transfer it to a large bowl.
5. For the hard sauce, in a bowl of an electric mixer, beat the butter until creamy. Add the sugar and vanilla, and beat until light and fluffy. Set aside.
6. Pour the ¼ cup whiskey over the pudding. Place a sugar cube in a large serving spoon and saturate it with the remaining tablespoon of whiskey. Hold a lighted match over the spoon to ignite. Pour the flaming whiskey and sugar on top of the pudding. When the flames subside, spoon the whiskey from the bottom of the bowl over the pudding and serve with the hard sauce. *Please note:* Before lighting the pudding, tie back your hair, have children leave the kitchen, and clear the workspace of all flammable objects. Do not light the pudding underneath cabinets or hanging objects.

✶ *Makes 12 servings*

Pudding Dessert

From the kitchen of Francine McCarthy

For the crust:

1 cup all-purpose flour
½ cup butter, softened
½ cup chopped walnuts

For the filling:

1 (8-ounce) package cream cheese
1 cup confectioners' sugar
1 large container Cool Whip
3 cups whole milk, cold
8 ounces instant pudding mix, chocolate, pistachio, banana, or vanilla
1 teaspoon vanilla extract
Optional fillings: bananas, raspberries, and chocolate
Optional toppings: chocolate sprinkles, sliced bananas, chocolate curls, Skor bars

1. Preheat the oven to 350°.
2. In a mixing bowl, combine the flour, butter, and walnuts. With a wooden spoon, beat until the mixture forms a crumbly dough.
3. Press into a 9 x 13-inch pan, and bake for 15 minutes. Set on a wire rack to cool.
4. In a large bowl of an electric mixer, beat the cream cheese until creamy. Add the sugar and 1 cup Cool Whip and mix well. Spread the cream cheese mixture over the warm crust.
5. In a large bowl, combine the milk, pudding mix, and vanilla. With a wooden spoon or hand-held mixer, beat until thickened. Evenly spread on top of the cream cheese mixture. Sprinkle optional fillings over the pudding mixture. Top with the remaining Cool Whip, cover, and refrigerate.
6. This can be made a day in advance. Garnish with additional toppings if desired and serve.

✶ *Makes 8 to 10 servings*

Pink Stuff

From the kitchen of Kellie Gould

My mom made this easy recipe for me and my two sisters throughout our childhood. Now, whenever there is a family gathering in Wisconsin and someone makes this creamy comfort food (which we call Pink Stuff because, well, it's pink), it immediately takes me back to being a young girl sitting around the dinner table with my sisters.

1 (8-ounce) container Cool Whip
1 (16-ounce) container small curd cottage cheese
1 (15-ounce) can crushed pineapple (slightly drained)
½ (3-ounce) package strawberry Jell-O
Maraschino cherries

1. In a large bowl, mix the Cool Whip, cottage cheese, crushed pineapple, and Jell-O together. Refrigerate for 1 to 2 hours.
2. Before serving, decorate the top with the maraschino cherries.

∗ *Makes 8 servings*

Baked Apple

From the kitchen of E.A.

My mother made this dessert when I was little. Sometimes she would fill the center with whipped cream, but I always preferred my warm apple filled with vanilla ice cream.

1 medium to large apple
¼ teaspoon butter
½ teaspoon brown sugar
¼ teaspoon cinnamon
Pinch of nutmeg (optional)

1. Preheat the oven to 350°.
2. Remove the core of the apple, leaving the bottom intact. Place the butter in the middle of the apple, and sprinkle with the brown sugar, cinnamon, and nutmeg.
3. Place the apple in a baking pan with ½ inch of water. Bake until soft, about 20 minutes.

✶ *Makes 1 serving*

Vanilla Sauce

From the kitchen of Elaine Kurschner

When we were kids we had warm vanilla sauce on our baked apples. They make the whole house smell so cozy and warm.

2 cups milk
2 egg yolks
2 tablespoons cornstarch
¼ cup sugar
½ teaspoon vanilla extract

1. In a heavy saucepan, whisk together the milk, egg yolks, cornstarch, and sugar until the sugar is dissolved. Place the pan over low heat, and, stirring with a wooden spoon, slowly bring to a boil. Remove from the heat, and continue to stir until thickened.
2. Add the vanilla, and serve warm over baked apples, pie, or cobbler.

∗ *Makes 2 cups sauce*

Ricotta Cream for Fresh Fruit

From the kitchen of Giovanna Roy

I love this recipe in the summer. It's a nice creamy dessert that is almost like pudding, but lighter and less fattening. I serve it with whatever fruit is perfectly ripe at the time. A mixture of strawberries, blueberries, and raspberries that have been sprinkled with a little sugar is wonderful with this. Just put the fruit in a little bowl and spoon the cream over it.

2 cups ricotta cheese
2 tablespoons milk or cream, if needed
⅓ cup sugar or to taste
1½ teaspoons vanilla extract
Grated zest of ½ orange
2 tablespoons Amaretto, Frangelico, Cointreau (or use orange juice), optional

1. In the bowl of a food processor, place the ricotta cheese, and pulse briefly. If the ricotta seems dry, add the milk and pulse until the cheese is almost smooth. Add the sugar and vanilla, and process, scraping the mixture from the sides of the bowl until perfectly smooth and satiny. Add the orange zest and the optional liqueur. Taste and adjust all of the flavorings.
2. Transfer the cream to a glass serving dish. Cover and refrigerate until thickened, at least 1 hour. Serve with fresh fruit.

✶ *Makes 2 cups cream*

Mom's Sauce for Strawberries

From the kitchen of Ginny Pigott

2 cups plus 6 tablespoons heavy cream
1 cup sugar
1 teaspoon unflavored gelatin
2 cups sour cream
1 teaspoon vanilla extract

1. In a heavy saucepan over low heat, combine the cream, sugar, and gelatin. Slowly cook, stirring, until the gelatin dissolves, about 5 to 10 minutes. Continue to cook until the sauce is thickened, about 3 to 5 minutes more. Remove from the heat.
2. Fold in the sour cream and vanilla. Mix well, and transfer to a bowl to chill or serve warm.

∗ *Makes about 1 quart sauce, enough for 4 pints of berries*

Aunt Gail's Hot Fudge Sauce

From the kitchen of P.V.

After my daughter was born, my husband's Aunt Gail cared for her when I returned to work. She provided such a loving environment for my daughter, for which I will always be grateful. After my younger daughter was born, I was fortunate to be able to leave work and be home full-time with my children. Aunt Gail continues to have a special relationship with my little girl and makes this wonderful sauce for her. She is a wonderful cook, and I don't think she would mind my sharing her recipe. This sauce keeps for quite a while in the refrigerator. Before serving, we put about a tablespoon per serving in a Pyrex cup and microwave it for about 15 to 20 seconds.

1½ squares unsweetened chocolate
¼ cup butter or margarine
¼ cup unsweetened cocoa powder
¾ cup sugar
4 ounces evaporated milk
Pinch of salt
½ teaspoon vanilla extract

1. In the top of a double boiler or a metal bowl placed over simmering water, melt the chocolate and butter. Stirring constantly, add the cocoa and sugar. Stir in the evaporated milk and salt, and stir until smooth. Remove from the heat.
2. Stir in the vanilla. It will thicken nicely when removed from the heat.

✶ *Makes 2 cups*

9

My Heirloom Recipes

Recipe name: ______________________________

From the kitchen of: ______________________________

Why I love this recipe: ______________________________

____

____

Makes: ______________________________

____

____

____

____

____

____

____

____

____

Recipe name: ____________________

From the kitchen of: ____________________

Why I love this recipe: ____________________

Makes: ____________________

Recipe name: ______________________________

From the kitchen of: ______________________________

Why I love this recipe: ______________________________

____

____

Makes: ______________________________

Recipe name: ______________________________

From the kitchen of: ______________________________

Why I love this recipe: ______________________________

____

____

Makes: ______________________________

Recipe name: ______________________________

From the kitchen of: ______________________________

Why I love this recipe: ______________________________

____

____

Makes: ______________________________

Recipe name: ______________________________

From the kitchen of: ______________________________

Why I love this recipe: ______________________________

____

____

Makes: ______________________________

Recipe name: ______________________________

From the kitchen of: ______________________________

Why I love this recipe: ______________________________

Makes: ________________________

Recipe name: ______________________________

From the kitchen of: ______________________________

Why I love this recipe: ______________________________

____

____

Makes: ______________________________

Recipe name: ______________________________

From the kitchen of: ______________________________

Why I love this recipe: ______________________________

____

____

Makes: ______________________________

Recipe name: ______________________________

From the kitchen of: ______________________________

Why I love this recipe: ______________________________

____

____

Makes: ______________________________

____

***

Metric Conversion Tables

By making a few conversions, cooks not accustomed to the U.S. measurement system can still make the recipes found in this book. Use the helpful charts below and on the next page to find the metric equivalents.

OVEN TEMPERATURE EQUIVALENTS		
FAHRENHEIT	**CELSIUS**	**GAS SETTING**
250	120	½
275	140	1
300	150	2
325	160	3
350	180	4
375	190	5
400	200	6
425	220	7
450	230	8
475	240	9
500	260	10

BAKING PAN SIZES	
AMERICAN	**METRIC**
11 x 7 x ½-inch pan	28 x 18 x 4-centimeter pan
13 x 9 x 2-inch pan	32.5 x 23 x 5-centimeter pan
15 x 10 x 2-inch pan	38 x 25.5 x 2.5-centimeter pan
9-inch pie plate	22 x 4- or 23 x 4-centimeter pie plate
9 x 5 x 3-inch loaf pan	23 x 13 x 6-centimeter or 2-pound narrow loaf pan
1½-quart casserole	1.5-liter casserole

LENGTH MEASURES	
⅛ inch	3 millimeters
¼ inch	6 millimeters
½ inch	12 millimeters
1 inch	2.5 centimeters

LIQUID AND DRY MEASURES	
U.S.	**METRIC (ROUNDED)**
¼ teaspoon	1.25 milliliters
½ teaspoon	2.5 milliliters
1 teaspoon	5 milliliters
1 tablespoon (3 teaspoons)	15 milliliters
1 fluid ounce (2 tablespoons)	30 milliliters
¼ cup	60 milliliters
⅓ cup	80 milliliters
1 cup	240 milliliters
1 pint (2 cups)	480 milliliters
1 quart (4 cups, 32 ounces)	960 milliliters
1 gallon (4 quarts)	3.84 liters
1 ounce (by weight)	28 grams
¼ pound (4 ounces)	114 grams
1 pound	454 grams
2¼ pounds	1 kilogram

Index

A

Adobo
Lolah Lazo's Adobo, 47
Pork Adobo, 46
All-Night Drop Cookies, 149
Amish Macaroni Salad, 70
Anise Biscotti, 150
Appetizers. *See also* Dips; Spreads
Bagel Chips, 22
Best Holiday Cheese Ball, 17
Cream Cheese and Pineapple Cheese Ball, 16
Festive Crostini, 23
Grandma Rosella's Haroset, 119
Nanny's Charleston Pickled Shrimp, 11
Nut-Stuffed Mushrooms, 13
Pizza Fondue, 18
Stuffed Jalapeños, 14
Stuffed Mushrooms, 12
Texas Caviar, 21
Apple cider
Overnight Apple French Toast, 6
Apples
Apple and Sweet Potato Casserole, 106
Apple Streusel Coffeecake, 8
Baked Apple, 202
Bubbe's Jewish Apple Cake, 174
Candy Apple Pie, 186
Grandma Patterson's Apple Crisp, 191
Grandma Rosella's Haroset, 119
Grandma Shoemaker's Cranberry Relish, 118
Old-fashioned Applesauce, 117
Applesauce
Applesauce Oatmeal Chocolate Chip Cookies, 148
Grandma Rose's Applesauce Cake, 175
Old-fashioned Applesauce, 117
Asparagus Luncheon Dish, 96
Aunt Audrey's Broccoli Casserole, 97
Aunt Gail's Hot Fudge Sauce, 206
Aunt Jewel's Chicken and Dumplings, 26
Aunt Mary's Pasta, 61
Aunt Sallie's Hot Potato Salad, 81

B

Bacon
Chicken Carbonara, 25
Creamy Sauerkraut, 99
German Potato Salad, 80
Grandpa Hubbard's Baked Beans, 91
My Dad's Baked Beans, 92
Stuffed Jalapeños, 14
Sweet and Sour Green Beans, 102
Bagel Chips, 22
Baked Apple, 202
Baked beans
Grandpa Hubbard's Baked Beans, 91
My Dad's Baked Beans, 92
Baked Chicken and Rice, 27
Baked Rice Fluff, 74
Balsamic Vinaigrette, 112
Baltimore Bride's Cake, 162
Bananas
Banana Oat Squares, 151
Granny Lewis's Banana Bread, 123
Bar cookies
Banana Oat Squares, 151
Chinese Chews, 152
Congo Squares, 153

Basic Tomato Sauce, 64
BBQ Kielbasa and Beans, 51
Beans
BBQ Kielbasa and Beans, 51
Grandpa Hubbard's Baked Beans, 91
My Dad's Baked Beans, 92
Pinto Beans with Salt Pork, 93
Sweet and Sour Green Beans, 102
Swiss Green Beans, 103
Beef
Basic Tomato Sauce, 64
Beef Pot Pie, 37
College Time Pot Roast, 38
Hungarian Goulash, 40
Mom's Beef Stew, 41
Mom's Beef-Vegetable Soup, 85
Plain Meatloaf, 35
Red Wine Pot Roast, 39
Spaghetti with Meatballs, 66–67
Spinach Lasagna, 65
Beer
Bratwurst, 52
Best Holiday Cheese Ball, 17
Biscotti
Anise Biscotti, 150
Biscuits
Mom's Biscuit Pudding, 196
Mom's Cloud Biscuits, 126
Southern Biscuits, 128
Black walnuts
Hog-Killing Cake, 171
Blackberry Cobbler, 190
Black-eyed peas
Texas Caviar, 21
Blueberries
Blueberry Tart with Cream Cheese Crust and Streusel Topping, 187
Mom's Blueberry Muffins, 131
Braised Pork, 42
Bratwurst, 52
Bread pudding
Menehune Bread Pudding, 195
Bread Salad, 111
Breads
Cinnamon Rolls, 127
Granny Lewis's Banana Bread, 123
Mom's Blueberry Muffins, 131
Mom's Cloud Biscuits, 126
Mom's Famous White Bread, 121
Myrtle's Butter Rolls, 130
Portuguese Sweet Bread (Masa), 122
Pumpkin Nutmeg Rolls, 129
Southern Biscuits, 128
Spicy Pineapple-Zucchini Bread, 125
Zucchini Nut Bread, 124
Breakfast dishes
Apple Streusel Coffeecake, 8
Christmas Coffeecake, 9
Cottage Cheese Pancakes, 5
Get Up and Go Breakfast Cookies, 10
Grits and Red-Eye Gravy, 4
Nona Rosa's Pepper and Egg Frittata, 1
Oven-Baked Spanish Omelet, 2
Overnight Apple French Toast, 6
Tomato and Egg on Toast, 3
Tried-and-True Sour Cream Coffeecake, 7
Bridge Cake (Kathy Cake), 161
Broccoli
Aunt Audrey's Broccoli Casserole, 97
Brownies
Old-fashioned Brownies, 154
Sand Art Brownie Mix, 155
Bubbe's Jewish Apple Cake, 174
Burnt Sugar Cake with Burnt Sugar Frosting, 164–65
Butter Crunch Toffee, 157

* C *

Cabbage
Cabbage Pudding, 98
Corned Beef and Cabbage Casserole, 36
Kapusta (Pork and Cabbage Stew), 45
Cakes
Baltimore Bride's Cake, 162
Bridge Cake (Kathy Cake), 161
Bubbe's Jewish Apple Cake, 174
Burnt Sugar Cake with Burnt Sugar Frosting, 164–65
Chocolate Chip Date Nut Cake, 176
Coconut Walnut Cake, 165
Grandma Rose's Applesauce Cake, 175
Grandmother's Strawberry Shortcake, 177
Great Aunt Helen's Peach Thing, 179
"Hog-Killing" Cake, 171

Italian Cream Cake with Cream Cheese Frosting, 168
Italian Rum Pastry Cake (Cassatta), 169
Ma-Ma's No-Bake Fruitcake, 180
Nanny's Japanese Fruit Cake, 166
Never-Fail Chocolate Cake, 163
One-Pan Chocolate Cake, 172
Poke Cake, 167
Poppy Seed Cake, 170
Pound Cake, 173

Candies
Butter Crunch Toffee, 157
Dad's Peanut Brittle, 156
Peanut Butter Fudge, 158
Ribbon Fantasy Fudge, 159
Tiger's Butter, 160

Candy Apple Pie, 186

Carrots
Beef Pot Pie, 37
Cheesy Potato Soup, 89
Copper Penny Salad, 113
Green Jell-O Salad, 115
Lolah Lazo's Pancit, 71
Mom's Beef Stew, 41
Mom's Beef-Vegetable Soup, 85

Casseroles. *See also* Main dishes
Apple and Sweet Potato Casserole, 106
Aunt Audrey's Broccoli Casserole, 97
Chicken Parmesan Risotto Casserole, 33
Corned Beef and Cabbage Casserole, 36
Granny's Squash Casserole, 105
Green Noodle Chicken Casserole, 31
Mom's Tuna Casserole, 57
Zucchini Casserole, 107

Cheese
Aunt Audrey's Broccoli Casserole, 97
Baked Rice Fluff, 74
Cheese and Potato Soup, 88
Cheesy Potato Soup, 89
Daddy's Mozzarella Chicken, 30
1886 Cheese Soup, 87
Grandmother's Macaroni and Cheese, 69
Green Noodle Chicken Casserole, 31
Homemade Manicotti, 63
1978 Sour Cream Enchiladas, 34
Pizza Fondue, 18
Pizza Loaf, 53
Spinach Lasagna, 65
Swiss Green Beans, 103
Taco Dip, 20
Zucchini Casserole, 107

Chicken
Aunt Jewel's Chicken and Dumplings, 26
Baked Chicken and Rice, 27
Chicken and Pasta, 32
Chicken Carbonara, 25
Chicken Paprikás, 28
Chicken Parmesan Risotto Casserole, 33
Daddy's Mozzarella Chicken, 30
Green Noodle Chicken Casserole, 31
Mom's Speedy Chicken Noodle Soup, 86
My Mom's Famous Chicken Squares, 29
1978 Sour Cream Enchiladas, 34

Chinese Chews, 152
Chinese Watercress and Meatball Soup, 83

Chocolate
All-Night Drop Cookies, 149
Applesauce Oatmeal Chocolate Chip Cookies, 148
Aunt Gail's Hot Fudge Sauce, 206
Bridge Cake (Kathy Cake), 161
Butter Crunch Toffee, 157
Chocolate Chip Date Nut Cake, 176
Congo Squares, 153
Granny's Pumpkin Cookies, 138
I Dare You to Eat Three of These Chocolate Chip Cookies, 142
Microwave Chocolate Pudding, 193
Never-Fail Chocolate Cake, 163
One-Pan Chocolate Cake, 172
Pam's Frosted Chocolate Nut Drop Cookies, 144
Ribbon Fantasy Fudge, 159
Sand Art Brownie Mix, 155
Stovetop Chocolate Pudding, 192
Tiger's Butter, 160

Christmas Coffeecake, 9
Cinnamon Rolls, 127
City Chicken, 48

Clams
Linguine with Clam Sauce, 68

Coconut
Coconut Cream Pie, 183
Coconut Walnut Cake, 165
Italian Cream Cake with Cream Cheese Frosting, 168

Coconut ***(continued)***
Nanny's Japanese Fruit Cake, 166
Ranger Cookies, 147
Sand Art Brownie Mix, 155
Cod with Tomatoes and Peppers, 54
Coffeecake
Apple Streusel Coffeecake, 8
Christmas Coffeecake, 9
Tried-and-True Sour Cream Coffeecake, 7
College Time Pot Roast, 38
Congo Squares, 153
Cookies. *See also* Bar cookies
All-Night Drop Cookies, 149
Anise Biscotti, 150
Applesauce Oatmeal Chocolate Chip Cookies, 148
Get Up and Go Breakfast Cookies, 10
Grandma's Sugar-Raisin Cookies, 145
Granny's Pumpkin Cookies, 138
Holiday Cut-outs, 139
I Dare You to Eat Three of These Chocolate Chip Cookies, 142
Lemon Crinkles, 140
My Mom's Pecan Crescents (Butter Balls), 133
My Mom's Whoppie Pies, 136–37
My Mother-in-law's Molasses Cookies, 141
Oatmeal Lace Cookies, 143
Orange Delight, 134
Pam's Frosted Chocolate Nut Drop Cookies, 144
Pecan Tassies, 135
Potato Chip Cookies, 146
Ranger Cookies, 147
Copper Penny Salad, 113
Corn
Cheese and Potato Soup, 88
Corn Pudding, 101
Corn, Zucchini, and Tomato Pie, 108
Fresh Corn Salad, 114
Fresh Cream-Style Corn, 100
Texas Caviar, 21
Zucchini Casserole, 107
Cornbread
Ma-Ma's Cornbread Dressing, 95
Corned Beef and Cabbage Casserole, 36
Cottage cheese
Cottage Cheese Pancakes, 5
Pierogies, 72
Pink Stuff, 201
Crab
Nanny's Crab Dip, 19
Cranberries
Cranberry Horseradish Relish, 120
Grandma Shoemaker's Cranberry Relish, 118
Cream cheese
Best Holiday Cheese Ball, 17
Blueberry Tart with Cream Cheese Crust and Streusel Topping, 187
Candy Apple Pie, 186
Cream Cheese and Pineapple Cheese Ball, 16
Festive Crostini, 23
Fruit Tarts, 188
Great Aunt Helen's Peach Thing, 179
"Hog-Killing" Cake, 171
Italian Cream Cake with Cream Cheese Frosting, 168
My Mom's Famous Chicken Squares, 29
Nanny's Crab Dip, 19
Pecan Tassies, 135
Pudding Dessert, 200
Spinach Feta Spread, 15
Stuffed Jalapeños, 14
Taco Dip, 20
Creamed Potatoes, 77
Creamy Sauerkraut, 99
Crustless Spinach and Feta Quiche, 104

⋆ **D** ⋆
Daddy's Mozzarella Chicken, 30
Dad's Peanut Brittle, 156
Dates
Chinese Chews, 152
Chocolate Chip Date Nut Cake, 176
Edwards Family Traditional Date Pudding, 197
Desserts
Baked Apple, 202
Blackberry Cobbler, 190
Edwards Family Traditional Date Pudding, 197
Grandma Patterson's Apple Crisp, 191
Menehune Bread Pudding, 195
Microwave Chocolate Pudding, 193
Mom's Biscuit Pudding, 196
Pink Stuff, 201
Plum Pudding, 198

Pudding Dessert, 200
Rhubarb Crisp, 189
Stovetop Chocolate Pudding, 192
Vanilla Pudding, 194
Dips
Nanny's Crab Dip, 19
Taco Dip, 20
Dressing
Grandma Edward's Oyster Dressing, 94
Ma-Ma's Cornbread Dressing, 95
Dumplings
Aunt Jewel's Chicken and Dumplings, 26
Chicken Paprikás, 28

* **E** *

Edwards Family Traditional Date Pudding, 197
Eggs
Amish Macaroni Salad, 70
Asparagus Luncheon Dish, 96
Aunt Sallie's Hot Potato Salad, 81
Baked Rice Fluff, 74
California-Style Egg Salad, 110
Crustless Spinach and Feta Quiche, 104
Egg Salad, 109
Ham and Pea Salad, 44
Lolah Lazo's Pancit, 71
Nona Rosa's Pepper and Egg Frittata, 1
Oven-Baked Spanish Omelet, 2
Overnight Apple French Toast
Tomato and Egg on Toast, 3
1886 Cheese Soup, 87
Enchiladas
1978 Sour Cream Enchiladas, 34

* **F** *

Festive Crostini, 23
Feta cheese
Chicken and Pasta, 32
Crustless Spinach and Feta Quiche, 104
Festive Crostini, 23
Shrimp in Tomatoes and Feta, 60
Spinach Feta Spread, 15
Fish
Cod with Tomatoes and Peppers, 54
Mom's Tuna Casserole, 57
Salmon Patties, 55
Fondue
Pizza Fondue, 18
French toast
Overnight Apple French Toast, 6
Fresh Corn Salad, 114
Fresh Cream-Style Corn, 100
Frosting
Baltimore Bride's Cake, 162
Burnt Sugar Cake with Burnt Sugar Frosting, 164–65
"Hog-Killing" Cake, 171
Italian Cream Cake with Cream Cheese Frosting, 168
My Mom's Decorator Frosting, 178
Nanny's Japanese Fruit Cake, 166
Never-Fail Chocolate Cake, 163
Fruit Tarts, 188
Fudge
Peanut Butter Fudge, 158
Ribbon Fantasy Fudge, 159

* **G** *

German Potato Pancakes, 76
German Potato Salad, 80
Get Up and Go Breakfast Cookies, 10
Grandma Edward's Oyster Dressing, 94
Grandma Patterson's Apple Crisp, 191
Grandma Rosella's Haroset, 119
Grandma Rosella's Potato Kugel, 79
Grandma Rose's Applesauce Cake, 175
Grandma Shoemaker's Cranberry Relish, 118
Grandma's Egg Noodles, 62
Grandma's Sugar-Raisin Cookies, 145
Grandmother's Macaroni and Cheese, 69
Grandmother's Strawberry Shortcake, 177
Grandpa Hubbard's Baked Beans, 91
Granny Lewis's Banana Bread, 123
Granny's Pumpkin Cookies, 138
Granny's Squash Casserole, 105
Gravy
Grits and Red-Eye Gravy, 4
Great Aunt Helen's Peach Thing, 179
Green beans
Sweet and Sour Green Beans, 102
Swiss Green Beans, 103
Green Jell-O Salad, 115
Green Noodle Chicken Casserole, 31
Grits and Red-Eye Gravy, 4

* H *
Ham
Grits and Red-Eye Gravy, 4
Ham and Pea Salad, 44
Lentil Soup, 90
Mother's Ham Loaf with Red Currant Sauce, 43
My Mom's Stuffed Potatoes, 78
Heirloom Rice and Sausage, 49
"Hog-Killing" Cake, 171
Holiday Cut-outs, 139
Homemade Manicotti, 63
Horseradish
Cranberry Horseradish Relish, 120
Hungarian Goulash, 40

* I *
I Dare You to Eat Three of These Chocolate Chip Cookies, 142
Italian Cream Cake with Cream Cheese Frosting, 168
Italian Rum Pastry Cake (Cassatta), 169
Italian Sausage with Peppers, 50

* J *
Jalapeño peppers
Stuffed Jalapeños, 14
Jason's Grilled Garlic Shrimp, 56
Jell-O
Green Jell-O Salad, 115
Pink Stuff, 201
Poke Cake, 167
Rhubarb Salad, 116

* K *
Kapusta (Pork and Cabbage Stew), 45
Kielbasa
BBQ Kielbasa and Beans, 51

* L *
Lasagna
Spinach Lasagna, 65
Lemon
Lemon Crinkles, 140
My Grandmother's Lemon Meringue Pie, 182
Nanny's Japanese Fruit Cake, 166
Lentil Soup, 90
Linguine with Clam Sauce, 68
Lolah Lazo's Adobo, 47
Lolah Lazo's Pancit, 71

* M *
Macaroni
Amish Macaroni Salad, 70
Grandmother's Macaroni and Cheese, 69
Main dishes. *See also* Casseroles
Asparagus Luncheon Dish, 96
Aunt Jewel's Chicken and Dumplings, 26
Baked Chicken and Rice, 27
BBQ Kielbasa and Beans, 51
Beef Pot Pie, 37
Braised Pork, 42
Bratwurst, 52
Chicken and Pasta, 32
Chicken Carbonara, 25
Chicken Paprikás, 28
City Chicken, 48
Cod with Tomatoes and Peppers, 54
College Time Pot Roast, 38
Crustless Spinach and Feta Quiche, 104
Daddy's Mozzarella Chicken, 30
Heirloom Rice and Sausage, 49
Hungarian Goulash, 40
Italian Sausage with Peppers, 50
Jason's Grilled Garlic Shrimp, 56
Lolah Lazo's Adobo, 47
Mother's Ham Loaf with Red Currant Sauce, 43
My Mom's Famous Chicken Squares, 29
1978 Sour Cream Enchiladas, 34
Pizza Loaf, 53
Plain Meatloaf, 35
Pork Adobo, 46
Red Wine Pot Roast, 39
Salmon Patties, 55
Shrimp Gumbo, 58–59
Shrimp in Tomatoes and Feta, 60
Ma-Ma's Cornbread Dressing, 95
Ma-Ma's No-Bake Fruitcake, 180
Mandarin oranges
Hog-Killing Cake, 171
Manicotti
Homemade Manicotti, 63
Maple syrup
Apple and Sweet Potato Casserole, 106

Marshmallows
Ma-Ma's No-Bake Fruitcake, 180
Meatballs
Chinese Watercress and Meatball Soup, 83
Spaghetti with Meatballs, 66–67
Meatloaf
Plain Meatloaf, 35
Menehune Bread Pudding, 195
Microwave Chocolate Pudding, 193
Mom's Beef Stew, 41
Mom's Beef-Vegetable Soup, 85
Mom's Biscuit Pudding, 196
Mom's Blueberry Muffins, 131
Mom's Cloud Biscuits, 126
Mom's Famous White Bread, 121
Mom's Matzo Ball Soup, 84
Mom's Potato Salad, 82
Mom's Pumpkin Pie, 184
Mom's Sauce for Strawberries, 205
Mom's Speedy Chicken Noodle Soup, 86
Mom's Tuna Casserole, 57
Mother's Ham Loaf with Red Currant Sauce, 43
Muffins
Mom's Blueberry Muffins, 131
Mushrooms
Best Holiday Cheese Ball, 17
Chicken Parmesan Risotto Casserole, 33
Green Noodle Chicken Casserole, 31
Nut-Stuffed Mushrooms, 13
Pizza Loaf, 53
Stuffed Mushrooms, 12
Wild Rice with Pecans and Mushrooms, 75
My Dad's Baked Beans, 92
My Grandmother's Lemon Meringue Pie, 182
My Mom's Decorator Frosting, 178
My Mom's Famous Chicken Squares, 29
My Mom's Pecan Crescents (Butter Balls), 133
My Mom's Stuffed Potatoes, 78
My Mom's Whoppie Pies, 136–37
My Mother-in-law's Molasses Cookies, 141
Myrtle's Butter Rolls, 130

* **N** *
Nanny's Charleston Pickled Shrimp, 11
Nanny's Crab Dip, 19
Nanny's Japanese Fruit Cake, 166
Never-Fail Chocolate Cake, 163
1978 Sour Cream Enchiladas, 34
Nona Rosa's Pepper and Egg Frittata, 1
Noodles
Grandma's Egg Noodles, 62
Green Noodle Chicken Casserole, 31
Mom's Speedy Chicken Noodle Soup, 86
Nuts. *See also* Pecans; Walnuts
Italian Cream Cake with Cream Cheese Frosting, 168
Old-fashioned Brownies, 154
Zucchini Nut Bread, 124
Nut-Stuffed Mushrooms, 13

* **O** *
Oatmeal
Applesauce Oatmeal Chocolate Chip Cookies, 148
Banana Oat Squares, 151
I Dare You to Eat Three of These Chocolate Chip Cookies, 142
Oatmeal Lace Cookies, 143
Ranger Cookies, 147
Okra
Shrimp Gumbo, 58–59
Old-fashioned Applesauce, 117
Old-fashioned Brownies, 154
One-Pan Chocolate Cake, 172
Oranges
Grandma Shoemaker's Cranberry Relish, 118
Nanny's Japanese Fruit Cake, 166
Orange Delight, 134
Oven-Baked Spanish Omelet, 2
Overnight Apple French Toast, 6
Oysters
Grandma Edward's Oyster Dressing, 94
Shrimp Gumbo, 58–59

* **P** *
Pam's Frosted Chocolate Nut Drop Cookies, 144
Pancakes
Cottage Cheese Pancakes, 5
German Potato Pancakes, 76
Pasta
Amish Macaroni Salad, 70
Aunt Mary's Pasta, 61
Chicken and Pasta, 32
Grandma's Egg Noodles, 62

Pasta ***(continued)***
Grandmother's Macaroni and Cheese, 69
Homemade Manicotti, 63
Lentil Soup, 90
Linguine with Clam Sauce, 68
Lolah Lazo's Pancit, 71
Mom's Tuna Casserole, 57
Pierogies, 72
Spaghetti with Meatballs, 66–67
Spinach Lasagna, 65
Peaches
Great Aunt Helen's Peach Thing, 179
Peanut butter
Peanut Butter Fudge, 158
Ribbon Fantasy Fudge, 159
Tiger's Butter, 160
Peanuts
Dad's Peanut Brittle, 156
Pears
Positively Pearable Pie, 181
Peas
Beef Pot Pie, 37
Chicken Carbonara, 25
Ham and Pea Salad, 44
Heirloom Rice and Sausage, 49
Mom's Beef-Vegetable Soup, 85
Pecans
Best Holiday Cheese Ball, 17
Candy Apple Pie, 186
Congo Squares, 153
Cream Cheese and Pineapple Cheese Ball, 16
Edwards Family Traditional Date Pudding, 197
Grandma Shoemaker's Cranberry Relish, 118
Granny's Pumpkin Cookies, 138
Ma-Ma's No-Bake Fruitcake, 180
My Mom's Pecan Crescents (Butter Balls), 133
Nanny's Japanese Fruit Cake, 166
Never-Fail Chocolate Cake, 163
Pecan Tassies, 135
Southern Pecan Pie, 185
Wild Rice with Pecans and Mushrooms, 75
Pepperoni
Pizza Loaf, 53
Peppers
Bratwurst, 52
Cod with Tomatoes and Peppers, 54
Copper Penny Salad, 113
Daddy's Mozzarella Chicken, 30
Hungarian Goulash, 40
Italian Sausage with Peppers, 50
Nona Rosa's Pepper and Egg Frittata, 1
Pizza Loaf, 53
Texas Caviar, 21
Pierogies, 72
Pies
Blueberry Tart with Cream Cheese Crust and Streusel Topping, 187
Candy Apple Pie, 186
Coconut Cream Pie, 183
Fruit Tarts, 188
Mom's Pumpkin Pie, 184
My Grandmother's Lemon Meringue Pie, 182
Positively Pearable Pie, 181
Southern Pecan Pie, 185
Pineapple
Cream Cheese and Pineapple Cheese Ball, 16
Green Jell-O Salad, 115
"Hog-Killing" Cake, 171
Ma-Ma's No-Bake Fruitcake, 180
Menehune Bread Pudding, 195
Pink Stuff, 201
Spicy Pineapple-Zucchini Bread, 125
Pink Stuff, 201
Pinto Beans with Salt Pork, 93
Pizza Fondue, 18
Pizza Loaf, 53
Plain Meatloaf, 35
Plum Pudding, 198
Poke Cake, 167
Poppy Seed Cake, 170
Pork. *See also* Sausage
Braised Pork, 42
Chinese Watercress and Meatball Soup, 83
City Chicken, 48
Hungarian Goulash, 40
Kapusta (Pork and Cabbage Stew), 45
Lolah Lazo's Adobo, 47
Lolah Lazo's Pancit, 71
Mother's Ham Loaf with Red Currant Sauce, 43
Pinto Beans with Salt Pork, 93
Pork Adobo, 46
Spaghetti with Meatballs, 66–67
Portuguese Sweet Bread (Masa), 122
Positively Pearable Pie, 181

Pot pie
Beef Pot Pie, 37
Potato Chip Cookies, 146
Potato salads
Aunt Sallie's Hot Potato Salad, 81
German Potato Salad, 80
Mom's Potato Salad, 82
Potatoes
Beef Pot Pie, 37
Cheese and Potato Soup, 88
Cheesy Potato Soup, 89
Creamed Potatoes, 77
German Potato Pancakes, 76
Grandma Rosella's Potato Kugel, 79
Mom's Beef Stew, 41
My Mom's Stuffed Potatoes, 78
Oven-Baked Spanish Omelet, 2
Pierogies, 72
Pound Cake, 173
Prunes
Plum Pudding, 198
Pudding
Cabbage Pudding, 98
Corn Pudding, 101
Edwards Family Traditional Date Pudding, 197
Menehune Bread Pudding, 195
Microwave Chocolate Pudding, 193
Mom's Biscuit Pudding, 196
Plum Pudding, 198
Pudding Dessert, 200
Stovetop Chocolate Pudding, 192
Vanilla Pudding, 194
Pudding Dessert, 200
Pumpkin
Granny's Pumpkin Cookies, 138
Mom's Pumpkin Pie, 184
Pumpkin Nutmeg Rolls, 129

*** Q ***

Quiche
Crustless Spinach and Feta Quiche, 104

*** R ***

Raisins
Grandma Rose's Applesauce Cake, 175
Grandma's Sugar-Raisin Cookies, 145
Ma-Ma's No-Bake Fruitcake, 180
Nanny's Japanese Fruit Cake, 166
Plum Pudding, 198
Zucchini Nut Bread, 124
Ranger Cookies, 147
Red Wine Pot Roast, 39
Rhubarb
Rhubarb Crisp, 189
Rhubarb Salad, 116
Ribbon Fantasy Fudge, 159
Rice
Baked Chicken and Rice, 27
Baked Rice Fluff, 74
Chicken Parmesan Risotto Casserole, 33
Heirloom Rice and Sausage, 49
Spanish Rice Dish, 73
Wild Rice with Pecans and Mushrooms, 75
Ricotta cheese
Homemade Manicotti, 63
Ricotta Cream for Fresh Fruit, 204
Spinach Lasagna, 65
Rolls
Cinnamon Rolls, 127
Myrtle's Butter Rolls, 130
Pumpkin Nutmeg Rolls, 129
Rum
Italian Rum Pastry Cake (Cassatta), 169

*** S ***

Salad dressing
Balsamic Vinaigrette, 112
Salads. *See also* Potato salads
Amish Macaroni Salad, 70
Bread Salad, 111
California-Style Egg Salad, 110
Copper Penny Salad, 113
Egg Salad, 109
Fresh Corn Salad, 114
Green Jell-O Salad, 115
Ham and Pea Salad, 44
Rhubarb Salad, 116
Salmon Patties, 55
Salt pork
Pinto Beans with Salt Pork, 93
Sand Art Brownie Mix, 155
Sauces
Aunt Gail's Hot Fudge Sauce, 206
Basic Tomato Sauce, 64

Sauces *(continued)*
Linguine with Clam Sauce, 68
Mom's Sauce for Strawberries, 205
Mother's Ham Loaf with Red Currant Sauce, 43
Ricotta Cream for Fresh Fruit, 204
Spaghetti with Meatballs, 66–67
Vanilla Sauce, 203
Sauerkraut
Bratwurst, 52
Creamy Sauerkraut, 99
Sausage
Basic Tomato Sauce, 64
Bratwurst, 52
Heirloom Rice and Sausage, 49
Italian Sausage with Peppers, 50
Pizza Loaf, 53
Shrimp Gumbo, 58–59
Stuffed Mushrooms, 12
Shrimp
Jason's Grilled Garlic Shrimp, 56
Lolah Lazo's Pancit, 71
Nanny's Charleston Pickled Shrimp, 11
Nanny's Crab Dip, 19
Shrimp Gumbo, 58–59
Shrimp in Tomatoes and Feta, 60
Side dishes
Apple and Sweet Potato Casserole, 106
Aunt Audrey's Broccoli Casserole, 97
Cabbage Pudding, 98
Corn Pudding, 101
Corn, Zucchini, and Tomato Pie, 108
Cranberry Horseradish Relish, 120
Creamy Sauerkraut, 99
Fresh Cream-Style Corn, 100
Grandma Shoemaker's Cranberry Relish, 118
Grandpa Hubbard's Baked Beans, 91
Granny's Squash Casserole, 105
My Dad's Baked Beans, 92
Old-fashioned Applesauce, 117
Sweet and Sour Green Beans, 102
Swiss Green Beans, 103
Zucchini Casserole, 107
Soup
Cheese and Potato Soup, 88
Cheesy Potato Soup, 89
Chinese Watercress and Meatball Soup, 83
1886 Cheese Soup, 87
Lentil Soup, 90
Mom's Beef-Vegetable Soup, 85
Mom's Matzo Ball Soup, 84
Mom's Speedy Chicken Noodle Soup, 86
Sour cream
Cheesy Potato Soup, 89
Chicken Paprikás, 28
Daddy's Mozzarella Chicken, 30
Green Noodle Chicken Casserole, 31
Mom's Sauce for Strawberries, 205
1978 Sour Cream Enchiladas, 34
Swiss Green Beans, 103
Taco Dip, 20
Tried-and-True Sour Cream Coffeecake, 7
Southern Biscuits, 128
Southern Pecan Pie, 185
Spaghetti with Meatballs, 66–67
Spanish Rice Dish, 73
Spicy Pineapple-Zucchini Bread, 125
Spinach
Crustless Spinach and Feta Quiche, 104
Spanish Rice Dish, 73
Spinach Feta Spread, 15
Spinach Lasagna, 65
Spreads
Spinach Feta Spread, 15
Squash
Granny's Squash Casserole, 105
Stew
Kapusta (Pork and Cabbage Stew), 45
Mom's Beef Stew, 41
Stovetop Chocolate Pudding, 192
Strawberries
Grandmother's Strawberry Shortcake, 177
Mom's Sauce for Strawberries, 205
Stuffed Jalapeños, 14
Stuffed Mushrooms, 12
Sun-dried tomatoes
Festive Crostini, 23
Sweet and Sour Green Beans, 102
Sweet potato
Apple and Sweet Potato Casserole, 106
Swiss Green Beans, 103

∗ T ∗
Taco Dip, 20

Tarts
Blueberry Tart with Cream Cheese Crust and Streusel Topping, 187
Fruit Tarts, 188
Texas Caviar, 21
Tiger's Butter, 160
Tomato and Egg on Toast, 3
Tomato sauce
Basic Tomato Sauce, 64
Spaghetti with Meatballs, 66–67
Tomatoes
BBQ Kielbasa and Beans, 51
Bread Salad, 111
Cod with Tomatoes and Peppers, 54
Corn, Zucchini, and Tomato Pie, 108
Daddy's Mozzarella Chicken, 30
Fresh Corn Salad, 114
Hungarian Goulash, 40
Italian Sausage with Peppers, 50
Kapusta (Pork and Cabbage Stew), 45
Mom's Beef-Vegetable Soup, 85
Shrimp in Tomatoes and Feta, 60
Spinach Lasagna, 65
Texas Caviar, 21
Tomato and Egg on Toast, 3
Tortillas
1978 Sour Cream Enchiladas, 34
Tried-and-True Sour Cream Coffeecake, 7
Tuna
Mom's Tuna Casserole, 57

∗ **V** ∗
Vanilla Pudding, 194
Vanilla Sauce, 203
Veal
Spaghetti with Meatballs, 66–67

∗ **W** ∗
Walnuts
Butter Crunch Toffee, 157
Chinese Chews, 152
Chocolate Chip Date Nut Cake, 176
Coconut Walnut Cake, 165
Grandma Rosella's Haroset, 119
Grandma Rose's Applesauce Cake, 175
"Hog-Killing" Cake, 171
I Dare You to Eat Three of These Chocolate Chip Cookies, 142
Nut-Stuffed Mushrooms, 13
Pam's Frosted Chocolate Nut Drop Cookies, 144
Potato Chip Cookies, 146
Pudding Dessert, 200
Sand Art Brownie Mix, 155
Spicy Pineapple-Zucchini Bread, 125
Tried-and-True Sour Cream Coffeecake, 7
Watercress
Chinese Watercress and Meatball Soup, 83
Wild Rice with Pecans and Mushrooms, 75

∗ **Z** ∗
Zucchini
Corn, Zucchini, and Tomato Pie, 108
Spicy Pineapple-Zucchini Bread, 125
Zucchini Casserole, 107
Zucchini Nut Bread, 124

***

About the Editor

Jennifer Saltiel is director of Parent Soup and the Food Channel for iVillage. She is also a cookbook author and freelance writer.

About iVillage

Based in New York City, iVillage Inc. was founded in 1995 with the mission of "humanizing cyberspace." In the early years of the Internet, there were few places for women to find solutions and discuss their problems, needs, and interests. By creating a clean, well-lit space, iVillage carved out a unique place where women could gather and find information and support on a wide range of topics relevant to their lives.

Today, iVillage is a leading women's media company and the number one source for women's information online, providing practical solutions and everyday support for women. iVillage includes iVillage.com, Women.com, Business Women's Network, Lamaze Publishing, the Newborn Channel, iVillage Solutions, Promotions.com, and Astrology.com. The backbone of iVillage is the network of Community Leaders who host thousands of message boards where women exchange practical solutions and find support on a daily basis.

iVillage.com's content areas include Astrology, Babies, Beauty, Diet & Fitness, Entertainment, Food, Health, Home & Garden, Lamaze, Money, Parenting, Pets, Pregnancy, Relationships, Shopping, and Work.